J. LeBron McBride, PhD

Spiritual Crisis
Surviving Trauma to the Soul

Pre-publication
REVIEWS,
COMMENTARIES,
EVALUATIONS . . .

"**O**nly one book in a thousand is worthy of reading every word, and repeatedly. Here is that book. I consider it one of the most worthwhile publications of our decade.

The author has studied wisely and well in the various fields bearing on his topic, and what he offers is pertinent, practical, and of exceeding value. The book is packed with illuminating insights and for most readers will prove far more valuable than a seeming eternity of counseling sessions.

Psychotherapist McBride draws from his own experience of denominational disillusionment and thereby demonstrates that there can be a significant harvest from the trauma of bitter loss. Both the pitfalls and the survival mechanisms associated with crisis are splendidly sketched, with both heart and head of the author interacting with reality."

Desmond Ford, PhD
President,
Good News Unlimited,
Manchester, England

"**S**piritual Crisis: Surviving Trauma to the Soul is a competent and comprehensive treatment of the nature and implications of spiritual crisis. The book reflects the heart of a sensitive and caring pastoral counselor who recognizes the importance of the spiritual in every aspect of life. This book will be instructive and uplifting to clergy, parishioners, and all mental health professionals who recognize the importance of caring for the soul."

E. Wayne Hill, PhD
Associate Professor,
Department of Family
and Child Sciences,
Florida State University

"**T**his book is both educational and inspirational. Its format renders it equally valuable as a text for professionals learning about crises, a reference for caregivers interacting with individuals in crises, and a treasury for those needing personal renewal and strength in their walk through life.

This is a comprehensive and caring resource written from the heart, and anchored by modern therapeutic literature. Its fruit is rooted in personal experience, fertilized by professional exposures, and harvested using a wide exposure to leaders in the field.

Dr. McBride insightfully identifies the core spiritual components of crises faced in life, and finds a balanced approach to not only surviving, but actually thriving through difficult times."

Wayne Dysinger, MD, MPH
Assistant Professor,
Dartmouth Medical School,
Hopkington, NH

"**M**cBride has brought together a number of valuable resources that will be especially helpful to pastors and spiritual care providers. This book is valuable just for its bibliography alone. The author's knowledge of the technical material of theology and psychotherapy informs the practice of ministry. It has taken years of integration for McBride to bring his wisdom to this reflective process of ministry. The challenge for those who read this book is to marinate in its offerings and reflect on its wisdom."

James A. Hyde, PhD
Associate Professor,
Director, Program of Ethics
and Pastoral Counseling,
Department of Psychiatry,
University of Louisville,
Kentucky

Spiritual Crisis
Surviving Trauma to the Soul

THE HAWORTH PRESS
Religion, Ministry & Pastoral Care

New, Recent, and Forthcoming Titles:

Growing Up: Pastoral Nurture for the Later Years by Thomas B. Robb

Religion and the Family: When God Helps by Laurel Arthur Burton

Victims of Dementia: Services, Support, and Care by Wm. Michael Clemmer

Horrific Traumata: A Pastoral Response to the Post-Traumatic Stress Disorder by N. Duncan Sinclair

Aging and God: Spiritual Pathways to Mental Health in Midlife and Later Years by Harold G. Koenig

Counseling for Spiritually Empowered Wholeness: A Hope-Centered Approach by Howard Clinebell

Shame: A Faith Perspective by Robert H. Albers

Dealing with Depression: Five Pastoral Interventions by Richard Dayringer

Righteous Religion: Unmasking the Illusions of Fundamentalism and Authoritarian Catholicism by Kathleen Y. Ritter and Craig W. O'Neill

Theological Context for Pastoral Caregiving: Word in Deed by Howard Stone

Pastoral Care in Pregnancy Loss: A Ministry Long Needed by Thomas Moe

A Gospel for the Mature Years: Finding Fulfillment by Knowing and Using Your Gifts by Harold Koenig, Tracy Lamar, and Betty Lamar

Is Religion Good for Your Health? The Effects of Religion on Physical and Mental Health by Harold Koenig

The Soul in Distress: What Every Pastoral Counselor Should Know About Emotional and Mental Illness by Richard Roukema

Spiritual Crisis: Surviving Trauma to the Soul by J. Lebron McBride

Spiritual Crisis
Surviving Trauma to the Soul

J. LeBron McBride, PhD

The Haworth Pastoral Press
An Imprint of The Haworth Press, Inc.
New York • London

Published by

The Haworth Pastoral Press, an imprint of The Haworth Press, Inc., 10 Alice Street, Binghamton, NY 13904-1580

The Haworth Press, Inc., 10 Alice Street, Binghamton, NY 13904-1580

Cover design by Marylouise E. Doyle.

Library of Congress Cataloging-in-Publication Data

McBride, J. LeBron.
    Spiritual crisis : surviving trauma to the soul / J. LeBron McBride.
        p.   cm.
    Includes bibliographical references and index.
    ISBN 0-7890-0460-7 (alk. paper).
    1. Pastoral counseling. 2. Pastoral psychology. 3. Spiritual life—Christianity. 4. Crisis intervention (Psychiatry) I. Title.
BV4012.2.M23 1998
253'.5—dc21   97-37273
                                                                                      CIP

To my wonderful children: Anna Marie and Benjamin. As I look into your precious little faces, I long to spare you from the crises of life. However, in the end, that would not be the best for you. So my wish is that your spiritual crises may truly become opportunities for growth.

ABOUT THE AUTHOR

J. LeBron McBride, PhD, an ordained minister, is Coordinator of Behavioral Medicine at the Georgia Baptist Family Residency Program in Morrow, Georgia. He is a licensed Marriage and Family Therapist and a clinical member and approved supervisor in the American Association of Marriage and Family Therapy. A member of several other organizations and author of numerous articles, he has served as a parish minister, pastoral counselor, and family therapist. His background in theology, medical education, and marriage and family therapy has given him a unique perspective from which to write *Spiritual Crisis.*

CONTENTS

Figures

Tables

Foreword

In the early part of this century the Reverend Anton Boisen, the founding parent of the clinical pastoral education movement, came upon a profound insight. Crisis, no matter what its source— emotional, physical, economic, or political—is always in some major way a spiritual crisis. For Boisen crisis always involved the destruction of meaning for the person experiencing the turmoil. When meaning fails (Who am I? What does God intend for me to do? Who is my neighbor?), we perceive ourselves to be in chaos: to be in a hell without the possibility of reason. For Boisen the cure for the crisis was a narrative process in which religion (or spirituality) puts a lid on chaos and the person experiencing it becomes a new person yet with continuity with the old.

J. LeBron McBride is an heir to Boisen's legacy and in turn he has given us our own inheritance as we read this book. All our crises, all our griefs, all our pains and struggles are spiritual in large part and neglect of this aspect of our lives—our psychosomatic, that is, our spiritual and bodily unity—will lead to continued mucking about in chaos. That is the message and gift of this book.

As with Boisen, the legacy of our spiritual crises and its cure was learned by Dr. McBride through three major avenues. First McBride knows of his own personal sojourns through spiritual crisis. His account of his crisis with his religious denomination in Chapter 6 is a moving description of a personal crisis that challenged his totality of understanding, his relationship with his friends and family, and finally his relationship with God. Mr. McBride is a "wounded healer." He has been there. He can be relied upon.

Second, Dr. McBride is a practitioner. He is a wise and gifted psychotherapist who, as he says in his introduction, has had the sacred opportunity of hearing people tell their stories. LeBron McBride has heard a call to care, and, when possible, to heal all sorts of people and their crises, large or small, acute or long lasting, debilitating or tempering. This second avenue is essential and gives the book credibility. He has been there not only in his own suffering and confusion but also as a witness to that of others. This is not only a sacred opportunity; it is also a sacramental practice because in the healing relationship one may find God.

Finally, McBride's third avenue is study. This is the disciplined reflection upon the "living human documents," as Boisen called the persons with whom he worked, using all the intellectual resources available to him. Dr. McBride has done his homework. The sources that he uses to help direct the content of this book reads like a who's who of modern psychology, pastoral care, and sociology. In his reflection upon life's spiritual crises McBride appeals to the tradition, to the researchers, and to the other reflective practitioners to strengthen his proposals and enlarge his and our experience.

This book has been written by a Christian theologian and caregiver. Though the author rightfully claims that non-Christians can profit from its content, as well they can, it is also directly aimed at those who are Christian and those whose history includes Christian principles and traditions, even though they may no longer identify with the organized church. I think that this is a strong point of this book. Unlike so many other books dealing with spiritual issues, McBride can claim that generic spirituality may, in the final analysis, not be foundationally spiritual at all. Authentic spirituality cannot be practiced apart from a spiritual community, be it the family or the church. Spiritual crisis, we learn, is always profoundly relational. This is most apparent in the last two chapters. In Chapter 13, we learn that a crisis of ethics is a crisis of how we are to be in relationship with others who may have contending interests. In Chapter 14, we learn that witnessing to crisis often becomes a dance of the healer and the one being healed, bringing both into peril as well as wholeness. I remember a comment made by a teacher of mine that seems relevant here. When this teacher/psychiatrist was asked how he knew if his patients got better he said, "That's simple. I know they are getting better because I am feeling better." Very little, if anything, in our lives happens in relational vacuums.

Finally, this notion of relationship and the traditions that guide relationships is embodied in this book. As God does not want us to be alone, nor should this book be read alone. Dr. McBride is absolutely consistent here. This book is to be read a little at a time, and then with the helpful questions for discussion at the end of each chapter, the reader is called to talk, amend, add to, and even rewrite the book always in communion with others. I see this book as one families can read together, and no doubt it will find a wide readership among those who study together as lay caregivers and as professional caregivers in churches and clinics.

It is an honor for me to recommend this book and to invite you forward into the wisdom, the care, and the humanity that awaits you. I read and shared this book with others as I went through my own spiritual crisis. This book helped me greatly during my time of trouble. Thank you, J. LeBron McBride.

Brian H. Childs, PhD
Professor of Pastoral Theology
Columbia Theological Seminary

Preface

J. LeBron McBride has done something I have never seen done before: he has brought together in one place the pertinent thinking about dealing with all kinds of life crises. And I do mean *all!* The fourteen chapters in this book range from the crisis of religious burnout to the crisis of working with persons in crisis and practically everything in between.

Ministers and therapists who deal every day with people in every conceivable kind of crisis will be delighted to have this work as a reference. For a quick read on the latest way to analyze and deal with the crisis at hand, one could not find a better resource.

Besides professionals who help others through crises, the book is excellent for the professionals themselves (dealing with their own crises) and for people who are going through crisis without professional help. It is readable and compassionately written and explicit in its information regarding the crisis at hand. Rather than owning many books on different crises one faces in life, a person can find a storehouse of knowledge and suggestions in this one book.

A very different emphasis of the book, as evidenced by the title, is on the spiritual aspect of each type of crisis. This is a truly unique contribution! Many crisis handbooks focus on the psychological or physical concomitants of crisis, but this is a first, of which I am aware, that considers the spiritual aspects. I am most grateful for this uniqueness.

Because Dr. McBride himself combines backgrounds in the ministry, therapy, and medical fields, he is uniquely qualified to compile a book combining wisdom from each of these sources. Those of us who work with people in crisis, including ourselves, will refer to this book over and over. *A real find!*

Kay Shurden, EdD
Associate Professor
Mercer University School of Medicine
Department of Psychiatry

Acknowledgments

This book owes its existence to those members of the churches I have pastored and the clients of therapy sessions I have counseled who have shared their intimate stories of crisis with me. To them I am thankful for what they have taught me about living, and at times, about dying. I have been honored to sit at the sacred temple of all types of circumstances and stressors and witness the spiritual struggles raised. I am amazed at the fortitude and strength of many of my church members and clients. They have taught me much.

I am especially appreciative of my wife, Deborah, and her support of this writing project. She endured far too many of my blank stares as I was engrossed in this book. Hopefully, my listening skills will return to normal as I send this off to the publisher.

I am indeed indebted to Kay Shurden for writing the preface and to Brian Childs for writing the foreword, as well as for making helpful suggestions as they read the manuscript. They were also very encouraging about the book. Kay and Brian are both extremely busy, yet took the time to assist me; I will be forever grateful to them. Lloyd Pilkington, who did a PhD counseling practicum under my supervision while I was writing this book, was also a source of assistance. He gave wonderful reflective and insightful comments to ideas I discussed with him.

Lastly, I thank my parents for the patient fortitude and the spiritual presence they instilled in me at an early age. Certainly, this book would not have been written without their early guidance. I have been blessed by many; I hope this book can be an instrument of blessing to those who read it.

Chapter 1

Introduction

The intensity of being a psychotherapist varies, but is often dramatic. In the course of a day a therapist may hear the stories of a woman who feels as if her heart has been ripped out because her son was recently murdered, a person who feels utterly betrayed since discovering an affair by a spouse, a person who has just been diagnosed with a chronic or terminal disease, and a person who has experienced the trauma of rape. Life breaks apart for such persons. Their pain cuts to the depths of their being. The world they once knew is gone. They are shaken to the very foundation of their beings. However, life does not require such dramatic events to create a crisis. Crisis may come as the proverbial "straw that broke the camel's back," or it may build gradually over several years to a critical point.

As I have had the sacred opportunity of hearing people tell their stories, over and over again I have witnessed profound existential questions and struggles come forth from the womb of such pain. In various languages, sometimes filled with religious jargon and sometimes filled with profanity, I have observed an emerging spiritual crisis. The core elements of the person's being and connectedness are pulled apart or stretched to the breaking point. The crisis is something much larger and deeper than mental, physical, or social disruption, although these are present also. Just as meat comes to the surface when a soup bowl is stirred, huge existential chunks of life come forward. I believe those who honestly struggle with these existential and spiritual issues eventually find healthier ways of living in the world than those who suppress them.

THE SPIRITUAL COMPONENT OF CRISIS

While there has been increased understanding of the impact of crisis upon our society and our individual lives, we are just beginning to consider crisis in terms of spirituality. Although it is probably not appropriate to separate physical, emotional, mental, and spiritual results of crisis, we do so at present because of our lack of ability to express these as a coherent whole. We do not have a good model for integrating all of these areas of life. The biopyschosocial model developed by Engels is helpful conceptually, but is difficult to implement on a practical level.[1] Hopefully someday we will have an adequate biopsychosocial *spiritual* paradigm that will assist us with better integration.

This book is an attempt to include the spiritual impact of crisis in the consideration of its effects. Although I have attempted to do this, I include the psychological, social, mental, and physical in my discussion. I only wish that I could better integrate all of these in some holistic manner. Figure 1.1 diagrams the interrelationships of the major areas of life experience. While many discuss these as necessary for a life balance, few note their feedback and influence upon each other.[2]

I have placed the spiritual at the center of the diagram to illustrate my belief that the spiritual core of a person is foundational. This core may or may not involve formal religion, but it does include the internal belief system a person maintains. It consists of the assumptive world or the basic lens through which the person filters thoughts and behaviors. For many it involves a consideration of relationship to a higher power, life force, or God. For me it is based upon a Christian approach and I have written from this perspective. However, I believe much of what I

FIGURE 1.1. The Synergistic Influences of Being

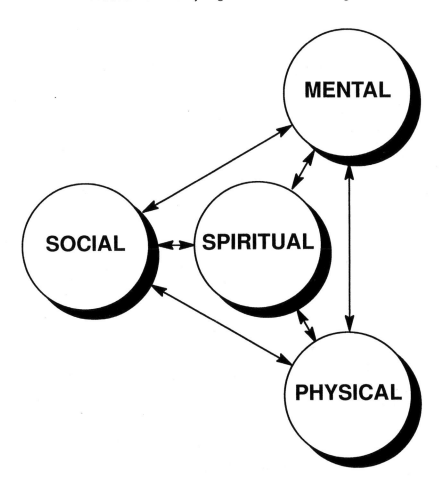

have written will be appropriate to persons of other orientations as well.

Just as scholars have alerted us to the critical transition points of both the individual and family life cycles, we need to think of critical points in spiritual life. Spiritual life is not just one great upward journey, at least not for most of us. We are influenced greatly by various events of life which have to be integrated into our belief structures or they become split off from our beings, resulting in unhealthy rebellion, denial, or apathy. Many honest seekers have turned away from the church and formal religion or, at least, have been puzzled by how their spiritual lives have not fit into the neat pattern so often presented of the faith journey.

Some may disagree with calling so many adjustments "crises," but this is the best term to describe what so often happens in life. Granted there are varying degrees of crisis; many of us do not experience the severity of crisis that I discuss in the second chapter, but our sense of coherence and faith in the continuity of life is shaken or shattered by many life events. While crises are often considered of short duration, this is not always the case. Some live in characteristic crisis states for years; some live in them intermittently.

SPIRITUAL CRISIS PATHWAYS

Spiritual Crisis Pathways: Protective and Preventive Measures

We might think of the impact of spiritual crisis as is diagrammed in Figure 1.2. However, these pathways are not to be taken as rigid paradigms; they are only suggestive and tentative. There are various ways spiritual crisis can come upon us. Our reactions depend upon many factors and contexts in our lives. While many spiritual crises are not preventable, some are. I hesitate to use a section for prevention and protection in Figure 1.2 because I do not want this concept to be used to judge those who have a spiritual crisis. Spiritual crisis can come to any of us no matter how many preventive or protective filters or barriers we may have in place. However, I do believe some lifestyle and existential ways of being may be protective, and certainly may assist us in coping with spiritual crisis. At the least, preventive measures may act as a lens through which crisis can eventually be seen in

FIGURE 1.2. Spiritual Crisis Pathways

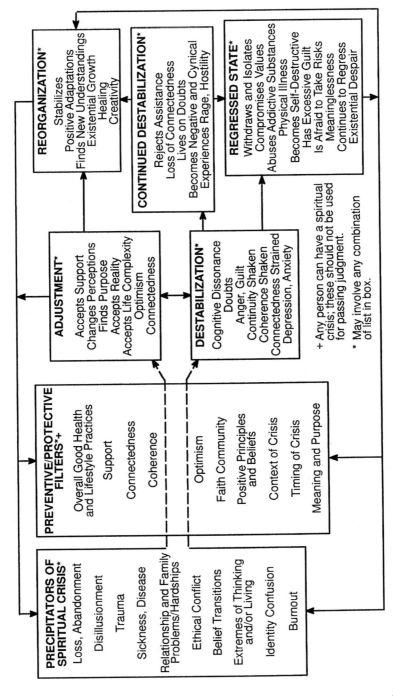

PRECIPITATORS OF SPIRITUAL CRISIS*

Loss, Abandonment
Disillusionment
Trauma
Sickness, Disease
Relationship and Family Problems/Hardships
Ethical Conflict
Belief Transitions
Extremes of Thinking and/or Living
Identity Confusion
Burnout

PREVENTIVE/PROTECTIVE FILTERS*+

Overall Good Health and Lifestyle Practices
Support
Connectedness
Coherence
Optimism
Faith Community
Positive Principles and Beliefs
Context of Crisis
Timing of Crisis
Meaning and Purpose

ADJUSTMENT*

Accepts Support
Changes Perceptions
Finds Purpose
Accepts Reality
Accepts Life Complexity
Optimism
Connectedness

DESTABILIZATION*

Cognitive Dissonance
Doubts
Anger, Guilt
Continuity Shaken
Coherence Shaken
Connectedness Strained
Depression, Anxiety

REORGANIZATION*

Stabilizes
Positive Adaptations
Finds New Understandings
Existential Growth
Healing
Creativity

CONTINUED DESTABILIZATION*

Rejects Assistance
Loss of Connectedness
Lives on Doubts
Becomes Negative and Cynical
Experiences Rage, Hostility

REGRESSED STATE*

Withdraws and Isolates
Compromises Values
Abuses Addictive Substances
Physical Illness
Becomes Self-Destructive
Has Excessive Guilt
Is Afraid to Take Risks
Meaninglessness
Continues to Regress
Existential Despair

+ Any person can have a spiritual crisis; these should not be used for passing judgment.

* May involve any combination of list in box.

5

an eternal perspective. Some reactions are unique and individual-ized for each person. The context in which a crisis occurs may also be preventive or protective of certain problems. For example, a person who experiences a financial loss because of a strongly held belief may experience a crisis, but may have a protective barrier because of the conviction of doing the right thing.

Precipitators of Spiritual Crisis

The chapters of this book examine some of the precipitators of spiritual crisis. These events can challenge our sense of safety, our belief system, how we perceive God, how we view the church, and how we feel in the world. The amount of pileup of these stressors can certainly also be a factor (see Chapter 3 regarding the ABCX Model). The challenge we are seeking to address is: the way we believe the world "should be" is shattered by crisis and trauma; a component of this is spiritual crisis.

Acceptance of Spiritual Crisis

In some cases individuals appear to adjust rather quickly to spiritual crisis. They remain optimistic or promptly regain an optimistic approach. They are able to gather and accept support and assistance from others as needed. Usually they can stabilize and reorganize and develop new perspectives to meet the crisis, to make meaning out of it, or simply accept it as a fact of life.

Destabilization and Regression as a Result of Spiritual Crisis

On the other hand, spiritual crisis can destablize to the point that individuals have tremendous internal conflict and disso-nance. Doubts about self, others, and God may be temporary or may be chronic. Anger and guilt may be overwhelming. Coher-ence and continuity may be lost or disturbed. Many individuals in spiritual crisis go through a period like this as a step toward eventual adjustment as described above. Others continue on a course of destablization to the point of becoming very withdrawn, with much negativity. Some regress even more to a self-destructive or apathetic mode with loss of meaning and connection. They can become very rigid in their constancy and inertia.

Reorganization and Growth During and After Spiritual Crisis

As seen in Figure 1.2, even those who have regressed to the extent just described can sometimes move toward reorganization and growth. It may be a particular event that transforms their perspective or an awakening that somehow slowly or dramatically develops. As the diagram indicates, there is feedback of information from experiences with spiritual crisis which may then influence preventive measures and usually affects our approach to future spiritual crises.

Biblical examples of these spiritual pathways can be easily found. We will briefly note only a few here. The story of Job is an example of a person who experienced horrific spiritual crisis. He went from great prosperity to poverty in a sudden and dramatic fashion. The theology common to his day saw suffering as punishment for sin, yet Job was a righteous man. He was not aware of any specific sins in his life and was, therefore, faced with the spiritual crisis of his theology not explaining the reality of his suffering. His friends were certainly no encouragement. Physical illness comes upon him to complicate matters even more. He maintains his integrity and faith in a remarkable fashion for awhile. Then comes a period of profound and continued destablization and discouragement. However, he is able to eventually adjust and reorganize. He finds new understandings and existential growth. He states his past following of tradition: ". . . Surely I spoke of things I did not understand . . ."[3] referring to his knowledge before his calamities. Now he has a more practical theology that assists him in better facing all the realities of life. Of course, according to the story, he had a little help from God in having his possessions restored many times over.

Another example is the profound spiritual crisis the disciples experienced at the time of the crucifixion. They were destabilized and were filled with depression, anxiety, fear, and doubt. Their continuity and coherence were shaken. We can suspect that all of the disciples struggled with a deep sense of guilt. The gospel stories give clear indications of this, particularly the disciple Peter. Yet eventually these very disciples had existential growth as a result of confronting the crisis instead of dissociating it. They were able to reorganize and develop new perspectives, and find new opportunities of faith. In many ways they were no longer the same persons as before the crisis. Judas, however, is an example of one who in spiritual crisis regressed to the profound existential despair of suicide. These are just a few of the many spiritual crises confronted clearly in the stories of scripture.

Many factors and contexts influence an individual's pathway when confronted with spiritual crisis. Our part is not to pass judgment on how he or she deals with the crisis or the pathway one travels, but to seek to understand better where the person is and what he or she needs from us. Having a basic reciprocal and flexible model that suggests a variety of pathways in dealing with crisis can assist us in not having a rigid concept of what is appropriate and normal in such circumstances. Throughout this book there is no attempt to "cookbook" a method of dealing with spiritual crisis. Instead I have attempted to take a broader approach which includes improving our understanding of precipitators of spiritual crises, thinking about these precipitators, and the wider influences that can be factors in spiritual crises.

TO WHOM THIS BOOK IS WRITTEN

This book is written for the caregiver who may be ministering to those going through crisis. Such caregivers may be ministers, pastoral counselors, church leaders, or therapists and counselors. It is also written for persons and their relatives and friends who are going through a crisis. Therefore, there is variation in the writing; sometimes it is written from the perspective of an educational reader for the professional, at other times as an educational reader for persons in crisis and their friends and family members. One caution: I would strongly recommend that those who do not have professional training or experience in working with severely traumatized persons obtain professional supervision for such work. The emotional components can be very powerful dynamics in this area of therapy.

The process of caregiving can be sacred ground. The care giver and the one cared for can become channels of grace for each other. By being with others in their pain we can stay in touch with our own struggles. In such settings we can sense the breaking of God's grace into our lives. Although often limited by me, I see my role as a caregiver as being a facilitator and supporter of God's grace. This means walking with persons through the darkest places in their lives. Caregiving offers a safe and accepting place for their struggles. Caregiving assists them in confronting the neglected or ignored areas of their lives. It helps them get in touch with their true selves and find what matters for them. It is offering faith, hope, and love so they can struggle toward wholeness. "Ultimately, healing and survival depend on existential categories: on vision, for example, on hope, on the imaginative capacity, on a response to challenge that treats crisis as opportunity for growth."[4] This is not a technique; it calls for grace and love.

INTRODUCTORY REMARKS

I consider this work to be introductory and brief in its treatment of each subject. It is certainly not the last word, but sometimes it will be the first such emphasis the reader will find on some of the topics. If the reader is somehow graced by this book, I will have accomplished my goal.

This book was written in my "spare time" away from my full-time employment while in the real world of wiping snotty noses, changing dirty diapers, and attempting to be supportive of a spouse in graduate school. I trust that this perspective has assisted me in keeping it practical and in touch with reality (at least most of the time). I am painfully aware of some of its contradictions, repetitions, and omissions. However, I have sought to bring together some of the lessons I have learned from my experience working in the fields of pastoral ministry, pastoral counseling, marriage and family therapy, and behavioral medicine. Parts of the book are clearly autobiographical; in other places the autobiographical is subdued, but often present. Hopefully, the reader will be able to benefit from my journey which, of course, continues. I write not as one who knows the way, but as a fellow traveler.

Questions for Discussion/Reflection

1. Do crisis points in life ultimately involve some spiritual dynamic?
2. Do you believe that each person has a spiritual core? If so, how would you define it?
3. What are some of the existential issues that you think are raised by crisis?
4. What are some of the resources that you believe assist a person in going through a crisis?
5. Have you known persons who became stuck in a crisis and did not move on with their lives? What do you think could keep a person stuck?

Chapter 2

The Crisis of Trauma

Traumatic events inflict wounds to the soul. Elie Wiesel wrote movingly of his terrible experience in the concentration camps. After seeing innocent children burned alive, he wrote, "flames consumed my faith forever" and that the experience "murdered my God and my soul."[1] Soldiers returning from Vietnam made such statements as, "I lost my soul in Vietnam."[2] Others have spoken or written of the experience of trauma as when "The spirit went numb"[3] and soul development is stopped,[4] and have called it a disorder of hope,[5] a spiritual night,[6] and a loss of wholeness.[7]

In this chapter we will examine the spiritual dynamics of trauma. Most of the chapter is about severe trauma and the resulting spiritual crisis and chronic problems. This will give us a sense of how we need to appreciate the extent of the trauma victim's crisis, and will assist us in understanding lesser traumas and the resulting stress reactions. At the end of the chapter, I apply the parallels between severe trauma and the more common traumas of our lives. Hopefully, this will give us a paradigm for understanding our own spiritual crises as well as those of others.

This chapter is largely taken from an article written by J. LeBron McBride and Gloria Armstrong titled "The Spiritual Dynamics of Post-Traumatic Stress Disorder" in *The Journal of Religion and Health,* Volume 34, No. 1, 1995, pp. 5-16. Copyright 1995 by Plenum Publishing Corp. Used by permission. An abridged version also appeared in Ridgeview Institute's *Insight Magazine,* Volume 17, No. 1, 1996.

TRAUMA DEFINED

A severe experience of trauma is defined as occurring when both of the following are present: "the person experienced, witnessed, or was confronted with an event or events that involved actual or threatened death or serious injury, or threat to the physical integrity of self or others" and "the person's response involved intense fear, helplessness, or horror."[8] A leading expert in the treatment of trauma defines the core of trauma in the following way:

> The essence of psychological trauma is the loss of faith that there is order and continuity in life. Trauma occurs when one loses the sense of having a safe place to retreat within or outside oneself to deal with frightening emotions and experiences.[9]

Post-traumatic stress disorder (PTSD) is the terminology used to describe those who have extended reactions to trauma. These reactions may even be delayed for years. Much has been written about PTSD in the last decade, yet relatively little has been written on the spiritual components of PTSD. However, Sinclair contended that "The most corrosive impact of horrific emotional trauma is to be found in the spiritual fabric of persons" and that "the condition of PTSD is spiritual at its deepest level."[10] Psychiatrist Joel Brende, who has written about PTSD and spirituality, says that unresolved symptoms of PTSD occur when survivors do not resolve their spiritual and emotional responses to stressful experience.[11]

THE IMPACT OF TRAUMA ON SPIRITUALITY

While there are no standardized tests to measure spiritual damage, no devices to correctly measure the effects of trauma on one's spirit, something does happen to the spiritual development of a person who is traumatized.

Many traumatized persons have felt the bonds and connections of life and belief tragically severed. Trauma made them feel cut off from God, from others and even from themselves. Individuals with chronic PTSD cannot trust; they cannot hope. They do not feel connected to their inner selves, much less to anyone else or God. Sinclair asks, "How can a viable spiritual life exist in the midst of all this? How can a connection with God be established in the midst of radical separation?"[12]

INSIGHTS INTO THE DAMAGE TO THE SPIRITUAL SELF

Winnicott vividly describes the concepts of the false self and the true self.[13] He defines the false self as that self that feels it has to conform to the expectations and feelings of others and denies or closes off its true feelings. The true self, on the other hand, is capable of experiencing its own feelings and needs as distinct from others.

This understanding of the true self hints at what Moore calls the soul when he refers to it as "not a thing, but a quality or a dimension of experiencing life and ourselves. It has to do with depth, value, relatedness, heart, and personal substance."[14] Soul appears, then, to be a concept of the self that speaks of the whole person integrated in his or her unique way. Trauma disrupts or destroys this integration of the total person. Dimensions of the self are disrupted by trauma which, while inclusive of the true and false self-concepts, may go even further. Charles Whitfield has written of a divine consciousness within each person which he calls the "higher self."[15] What happens to this higher self or soul as a result of trauma? It appears that the energy and creative and powerful force for living that some associate with spirituality[16] is often blocked in the life of the traumatized person.

Bradshaw describes the false self as the "wounded self."[17] It certainly appears to be characteristic of chronic PTSD patients that a wounded self or soul lies at the very core of their being. As a result, they often have a profound sense of spiritual alienation and emptiness. Masterson's term "abandonment depression"[18] actively describes such victims of unresolved trauma. They seem to go through life with the words from the Judeo-Christian heritage: "My God, my God, why have you forsaken me?" upon their lips.

Abandonment extends in many cases to the point where the person feels forsaken and abandoned by absolutely everyone else as well. Brende suggests that chronic PTSD is likely to occur when survivors feel isolated, abandoned by would-be protectors, or betrayed.[19] The self is profoundly alone; the connectedness between self and others is broken. "The victim is left with a view of the self which is either damaged, contaminated by the humiliation, pain, and fear that the event imposed, or a fragmented sense of self."[20]

Those who experience trauma have their world turned upside down. How can the event be integrated into their belief system? Many find themselves totally disoriented and unsure of what they believe. They undergo a severe crisis of faith in which it becomes difficult to separate good from evil; the boundary is no longer there.

While some professionals have been hesitant to use the word "evil," writers on trauma are beginning to now use this term. Many traumatized patients certainly use it. Carl Jung tells us that "on the question of good and evil the psychotherapist is brought shoulder to shoulder with the clergyman."[21]

The dichotomy of good and evil becomes more and more intense in the traumatized person, the splitting process increasingly extreme in its effects. It appears, then, that the term "evil" is appropriate as being descriptive of the worst one can perceive or experience. In object relations terms, a traumatized person has introjected a flood of bad objects, often to the point where a patient will say: "I am evil." It is as though "good" were expelled entirely from the individual's personal experience. There is no soothing object to bring comfort and constancy. There is no sense of security, no hope of redemption. This profound feeling of badness or evil is one of the most powerful signals that the soul of the person has been disturbed.

The belief that one is evil at the core is the aspect most often presented by chronic PTSD patients who are most resistant to change. Even after some have been in therapy for years, have learned to manage the lingering symptoms of chronic PTSD, and are functioning at a reasonably high level, the belief that they are evil and that all progress is a sham may continue to create an internal warfare.

Persons with such trauma of soul cannot find peace. They lack positive direction. Traditional modes of finding peace and contentment seem to remain unavailable to them. The hyperarousal and lack of anxiety modulation make it impossible for the spiritual disciplines of reflection, meditation, prayer, and communion to provide much relief. The result, for many, is a swing to dangerously extreme forms of living.

Pynoos has written about the impact of trauma on a child's development: "Consequently, there may be interference with the emergence of moral concepts, resulting in behavior that is overly regulated by considerations of good or bad or, alternatively, manifestly amoral."[22] This certainly points to a disturbance of the soul and its rough effects on spirituality.

Marmar and others speak of PTSD patients alternating between states of overcontrol and undercontrol.[23] Many become desperate in their attempt to control and become very rigid and perfectionistic. Spontaneity is lost. This may play out in more controlling and rigid forms of religion, which may then be used as a replacement for self and spirituality instead of as a tool for spiritual development. One of the dangers is that religion itself may also become traumatizing through extreme conformity and control, thus adding all the more to the loss of selfhood.[24] On the other hand, certain aspects of religion may offer the very structure the traumatized person needs in order to function and find some containment for their anxiety. More expressive forms of religion may give a person access to parts of the split-off affective self.

Others give up attempts to control themselves, yielding to their impulses. Their belief-systems are so shattered that they cannot seem to pull them back together again. They look for relief from the intensity of the trauma and the associated powerlessness and emptiness in the quickest way possible. Addiction is often a result. As Solomon has written in another context: "Drugs give the feeling of omnipotence, of perfection, of driving away the destructive or empty core self."[25] Drugs certainly seem to have the attributes of omnipotence, miraculously shutting down the overwhelming pain even though this proves a pseudo relief in the long run. Addictions provide a pseudo spirituality and counterfeit at the eventual cost of more destruction to the self.

PASTORAL TREATMENT CONCERNS

A useful framework for the holistic treatment of persons with PTSD takes into account the spiritual dynamics described above. The structure might be thought of in terms of "The Eight Rs" of recovery from chronic PTSD as shown in Figure 2.1. These phases should not be thought of as mutually exclusive or as always proceeding in linear fashion. Rather, the phases sometimes form a spiral cycling back to previous stages in the course of treatment.

THE RISKING AND REVEALING PHASE

Winnicott uses the term "holding environment" to refer to the role of the caretaker and the safe milieu of care for the young

FIGURE 2.1 The Eight Rs of Trauma Recovery

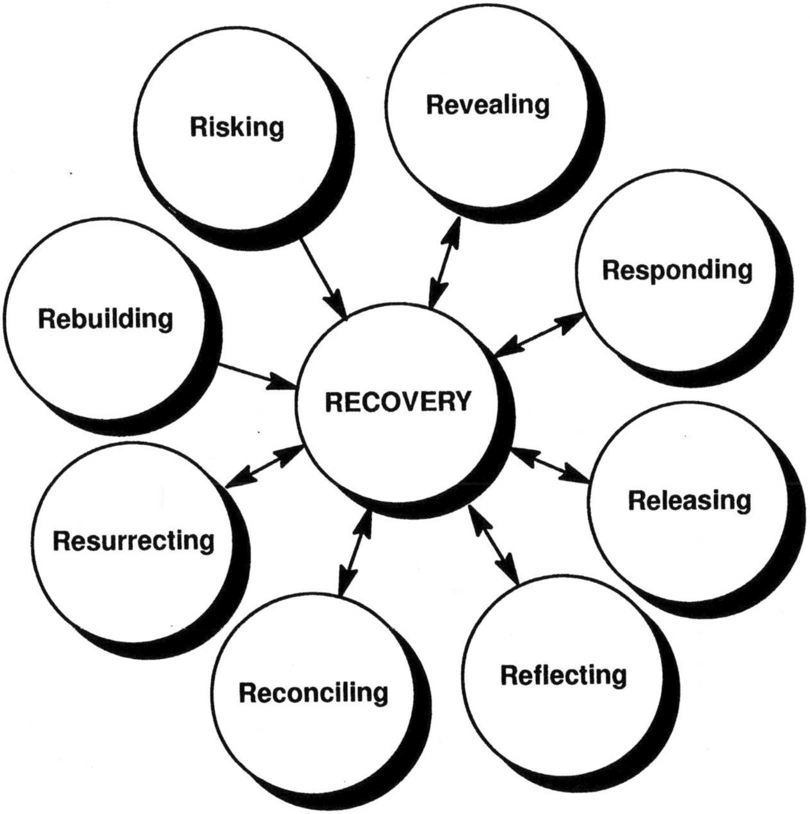

child. The appropriate holding environment provides the nurturance and safety needed for the exploring child to grow and develop in a healthy way. Therapists have also used this term to discuss the safety and nurturance of the therapy hour. This is of particular relevance in work with persons suffering from chronic PTSD and its impact on their spirituality. It is a great risk for them to begin to trust another person and also to be known in therapy. Their need for safety in therapy is always of utmost importance.

The engagement process between therapists and chronic PTSD patients is usually gradual and slow. Patients trust no one, or are at the least, suspicious and guarded. The safe holding environment has to develop at the patient's speed. Rushing the process is likely to push them away from therapy, confirming once more their conviction that no one can be trusted.

A gradual, structured, and thorough history-taking can provide some initial safety. The emphasis in the beginning is on the facts of the patient's life. The trauma may or may not be addressed at this time depending upon the patient's previous experience with therapy. We include the religious and spiritual history of patients as a part of their overall history. Additionally, their family and relationship history may give us insights into how the trauma has affected their connectedness with others. This history-taking often gives clues to some of the existential issues our patients are facing.

There may be an "affect lameness"[26] during this initial engagement process, but it is best not to address this unless it is clearly indicated. The PTSD patient needs to feel safe before discussing his or her deepest emotions. In the beginning we are simply seeking to make the therapy room a place the patient can trust. It is interesting that many religious metaphors are related to safety and trust. For example, in the Judeo-Christian tradition God is referred to as a refuge, a shepherd, a cleft in the rock. Safety is an important foundation for spiritual development and growth as well as for recovery from the spiritual arrest that occurs with trauma.

Once safety has been established, chronic PTSD patients need to tell their stories, to gradually reveal the secrets. These patients often have a history of literally hiding from abusers, which has led to a psychological hiding from others as well.[27] This is a very difficult phase of therapy for most of them. One middle-aged patient was afraid to tell family secrets for fear her mother would attack her. This fear was internalized in early childhood and persisted, even though her mother had died several years before the patient's therapy began. The majority of persons traumatized by incest in childhood, according to Judith Herman, reach adulthood with their secret intact.[28] We suspect this is also true for those who have been traumatized during childhood in other ways as well. When secrets are kept with such determination, a "dead zone" develops in the psyche that works like an anesthetic to cut individuals off from those who would give love and protection.[29]

Often these secrets are about the trauma and the impact it has had upon patients' view of religion, God, or others. The trauma may have precipitated a spiritual night in which they have lost their faith in a God who would protect or rescue them. This spiritual loss may become a major subject of treatment. Another way a patient may be struggling spiritually is by interpreting trauma as a punishment from God. Faith in humanity can also be lost, resulting in alienation from almost everyone.

There is something in the risking and revealing with a trusted person that is very healing to PTSD patients. The therapeutic holding environment allows them to become known as persons, perhaps becomes the first place where they have been known and not used. While this is a frightening experience, it is also a validating one.[30]

THE RESPONDING AND RELEASING PHASE

Until the trauma story is told and the emotions reconnected, a person is often spiritually arrested developmentally, and has difficulty looking at spiritual issues from any other focus than the one that was present when the trauma occurred. During this time, an accepting holding environment must be provided in which the patient can confront all the feelings, emotions, and thoughts that he or she fears others might condemn. This nonjudgmental and tolerant aspect of counseling is of utmost importance if true healing is to occur. "A wound is not disinfected once and then forgotten, but is tended to and washed several times while it heals."[31]

Chronic PTSD patients have shut off the affective components of their trauma and must gradually integrate them now with the support of therapy. Emotions eventually become part of their story. Rage, hostility, panic, despair, and other feelings surface. This may be difficult for the patient and therapist alike and requires clear communication and a calming, concerned attitude from the therapist. The patient has believed that these intense feelings would destroy them or others if released, and that no one could endure the exposure to them. It is important for split-off emotions to finally be accepted and released. The therapist fosters healing by not withdrawing from the patient's terrifying emotional world.

THE REFLECTING AND RECONCILING PHASE

Moore, referring to an incest survivor who remained focused on the incest as her primary identity, concludes: "but her story needed to be deepened, perceived in a more complicated manner, and reflected upon from many points of view, not only from the one that said: if you have experienced this, then you will be forever damaged."[32] This reflection takes time, a safe holding environment, and a trusted therapist or friend.

Just as an infant uses the caretaker as a "beacon of orientation,"[33] the PTSD patient can use counseling as a "beacon of orientation" to move toward meaning and wholeness. The holding environment of counseling gradually becomes a safe place for the patient to explore the trauma's meaning and integrate it into his or her life.

For Krystal, the meaning the PTSD patient gives to the trauma may be more important than the intensity of the trauma.[34] Carl Jung believed that the suffering which we cannot endure is that which has no meaning. For him the theories of Freud and Adler fail because they are concerned with drives and not with the spiritual needs of the patient and thus do not give meaning to life.[35]

Patients have to find some way to assess and struggle with the meaning they give to trauma. This does not mean that the trauma can be explained, but that the patient's worldview can begin to include events that harm innocent persons. The reconciling of the trauma in this way is quite different from believing the victim is evil or the cause of the trauma.

THE RESURRECTING AND REBUILDING PHASE

As healing progresses, the narrow focus that so often occurs with trauma broadens. Bradshaw calls this a "spiritual awakening" and a "growth and expansion of awareness."[36] Pearsall refers to ancient spiritual healers who defined illness as being trapped in one level of reality and saw healing as a restoring of the ability to experience all levels of the reality of their spirit.[37] This is a fitting description both of the myopic focus caused by trauma and the way true recovery broadens perspectives on the experience of living. This is the phase in which a patient may begin to be able to experience the transcendent, the mystical, and the existential aspects of life.

This expansion of awareness must include an integration of the good and the bad in the patient, others, and the world. The extreme polarities have to be seen for what they are: extreme views of living.

Another area of expansion for the chronic PTSD patient, once the fear of contaminating others has lessened and the patient has developed some level of trust, is that of moving from a stance of isolation to one of reengaging friends and family. This is a sign of movement toward wholeness and is an energizing force as well. Pearsall stresses the importance of his family's love in his recovery from physical illness as stabilizing his spirit in much the same way high-tech medicine stabilized his body.[38] Family and social relationships are also vital for the person rebuilding from chronic PTSD. This connectedness part of treatment must not be overlooked, because its powerful healing potential and its effect upon spirituality go well beyond what psychotherapy alone can provide. As Yalom counseled one of his patients "the times you've been most persistently depressed are the times you've broken your connections to everyone and been really isolated. There's an important message in there—about keeping your life peopled."[39]

Cognitive counseling interventions may be useful during the resurrecting and rebuilding process in addressing the distorted thinking and assumptions of chronic PTSD patients about themselves and others, spirituality, and God. Often they have built elaborate structures of thought and feeling upon faulty worldviews that support their views. A reframing of religious ideas may now be possible.

With treatment there gradually comes a movement toward integration. To use theological terms, it is a kind of resurrection. Through telling the story and being heard, grieving and feeling the pain with a trusted person, reconnecting and integrating occur and the chronic PTSD patient is resurrected from the "dead zone."[40]

APPLICATION TO THOSE WITH LESS SEVERE TRAUMA

I hope many of us will never experience the extent of trauma and the chronically painful and intense reactions just described. However, there is certainly a better than average chance that we or a friend or family member will experience some form of trauma. Therefore, being aware of the issues involved should be of interest to all.

Also, by examining the extreme cases we can learn more about our reactions to the lesser traumas of life. Even if our lives are not threatened by serious injury to ourselves or others, we live in a world in which threats to our physical, spiritual, social, and emotional integrity occur at various levels. Our sense of order and safety is often battered by the stressors of life.

Such events may challenge our faith, raise questions we have never thought previously, and release emotions much more intense than usual. It is important during such times for us to find a trusted friend or counselor for support and to keep us oriented. While we will not usually continue to have such thoughts and feelings on a chronic basis as the PTSD patients described earlier, we may have some of the same symptoms for awhile.

We should not see such struggles as spiritual failures, but as spiritual and emotional adjustments as we live in the world. We may struggle with a feeling of loss of God and be unable to meditate, read, and pray, as well as have an inability to reflect on matters of the spirit. In such cases, we are simply experiencing the spiritual dynamics of the traumas of our lives. During such times we need a sense of community or connection with at least one person to guide us through. It may be a precarious clinging to God that carries us: "Even though I walk through the valley of the shadow of death, . . . you are with me."[41] In the shadow times God may be temporarily eclipsed from our view, but is still with us.

The remainder of this book deals with some of the major transitions and conditions that can bring trauma or crisis of one degree or another to our lives. Often it may be important for the reader to reflect upon the material in this chapter as a basis of how crisis and trauma impact our lives. I encourage you to consider how "The Eight Rs" of recovery: risking and revealing, responding and releasing, reflecting and reconciling, and resurrecting and rebuilding may be useful in your own recovery from the crises in your life.

Questions for Discussion/Reflection

1. Whom have you known who has experienced a severe trauma? How did it affect that person's life?

2. How well do you think your faith community ministers to those who have been traumatized?
3. Have you ever heard someone speak as though the recovery from trauma should occur if one would only pray enough or have enough faith?
4. Do you think the parallels made in this chapter between severe trauma and the "traumas" of our daily lives are appropriate?
5. What traumas of daily living do you think are impacting our society?

Chapter 3

The Crisis of Relationship and Family Problems

I chuckle as I recall the opening words of my very first sermon in a class on preaching years ago. The words were: "We live in a world of broken and distorted relationships. . . ." I chuckle because I remember going over and over the words of the sermon in my anxiety about preaching to my classmates. Although I doubt I would begin a sermon with the same words today, unfortunately the opening words of that sermon ever ring true. The crisis that is precipitated by dysfunctional and broken relationships can be the most severe of all.

Stephen Covey begins a chapter in one of his books by having readers imagine they are at their own funeral and what they would like to have said by the funeral speakers.[1] Upon first reading this I thought it rather morbid. However, it does help one focus on what is really important. Most of us would want to be remembered as being good mothers or fathers, spouses, or friends. Relationships are what give us the greatest happiness and sometimes the greatest pain.

In this chapter we will explore some of the ways our families teach us about God, and Judeo-Christian beliefs teach us about relationships and families. Next we will look at the basic needs and current faults with relationships and families. A theological model for family relationships will be described.

THE ANTHROPOMORPHISM OF GOD

We use human (anthropological) descriptions to talk about God since this is our perspective and view of the world. We speak of God and visualize God in human terms. There is nothing wrong with using human terms to describe God as long as we realize the limitations of human words to really describe a God who is far beyond our human language. This is also the tradition of scriptures and, of course, we have the central Christian belief of the incarnation of God in human form in Jesus Christ.

PARENTS AS GOD IMAGE

The earliest images we have of God are usually associated with images of our parents. This becomes a very humbling thought once we have children and we realize its limitations. James and Melissa Griffith use the term "God-construct" to describe the mental perception and private image a person has of God.[2] They suggest that God-constructs or schemas organize and determine how a child will respond to perturbations in life. The Griffiths believe that there may or may not be clear parallels between a person's God-construct and his or her doctrinal beliefs. They propose that an important part of the God-construct is the conversation that emerges internally between a person's God-construct and the self. These conversations may impact greatly on a person's life and the solutions a person attempts. This is graphically presented in Figures 3.1 and 3.2.

Thus is it not difficult to suppose that early relationships affect our God-construct as well as our relationship with God, our later relationships with others, and the way we view life.

> Beliefs are intertwined with the relationships we have had, now have, or would like to have, with others whom we love and whose lives matter decisively. Internal representations of these significant others constitute some of our most important "object relations," and holding on to certain beliefs is a way of maintaining those relations.[3]

FIGURE 3.1. Drift of the God-Schemes (Positive)

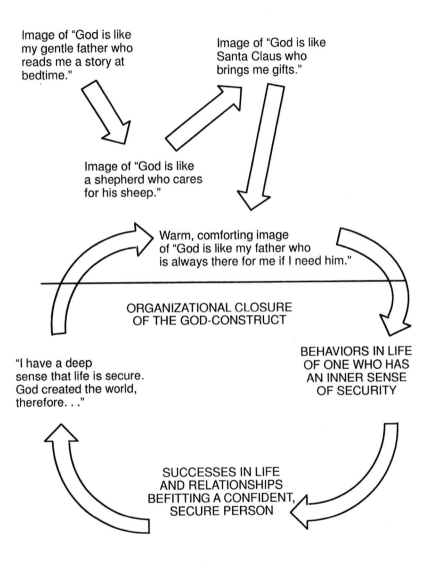

Source: James and Melissa Griffith, Therapeutic Change in Religious Families: Working with the God-Construct. In *Religion and the Family: When God Helps*, Laurel Burton, Editor, The Haworth Press, 1992, p. 68. Used by permission.

FIGURE 3.2. Drift of the God-Schemes (Negative)

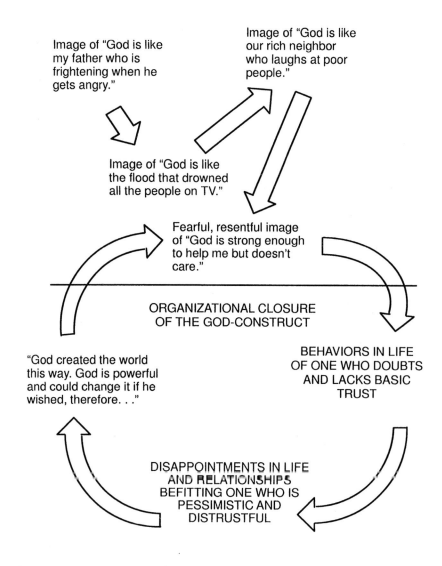

Source: James and Melissa Griffith, Therapeutic Change in Religious Families: Working with the God-Construct. In *Religion and the Family: When God Helps,* Laurel Burton, Editor, The Haworth Press, 1992, p. 69. Used by permission.

Cooper, writing about the work of Bradshaw, states of a negative God-construct: ". . . we are assuming that God is saying "no" to our being. We then project this self-condemnation onto God and assume that it constitutes God's opinion of us as well. We *feel* unworthy, so we assume that we *are* unworthy."[4] Such God-constructs can precipitate spiritual crises in our belief world.

FAMILY DYNAMICS AS GOD IMAGE

Many theories of psychology and human development point to the early years of a person's life as crucial. "It is generally understood that the nature of and the quality of the child's relationships with parents during the first several years will critically determine the major features of the child's—and later the adult's—relationships with others."[5] Object relations theory postulates that our basic patterns and instruction manual for living comes into existence in the context of relationship.[6] Whereas Freud saw human motivation and development as based upon biological needs and drives, object relations theorists have seen the main motivation of humans as a desire for relationship. Fairbairn stated that the earliest, deepest wish is for a loving, satisfying connection with a nurturing parent and that the need for a satisfactory relationship constitutes the fundamental motive in life.[7]

We are born with a need for attachment that does not go away. From a theological orientation, this need for attachment can be seen as spiritual since the spiritual includes connectedness in relationships. It also involves our need for attachment to God. In theological language one aspect of the Image of God that has survived the fall is the need and desire for relationships. "That children have an early awareness of a fantasy object capable of satisfying their hunger may be evidence of the Imago Dei *(Image of God)* in fallen humanity."[8] This is why we can speak of sin as the breaking of relationship or connectedness.

Object relations theory states that as children, we all form internal versions (introjects) of the important persons in our lives.[9]

"The internal object relations function as a kind of template that determines one's feelings, beliefs, expectations, fears, wishes, and emotions with respect to important interpersonal relationships."[10] Therefore, the emotional systems we experienced in reality or from our perspective of reality can strongly influence not only our relationships, but our functional beliefs.[11]

Many factors enter into these introjects and they, of course, do not always match with true reality. In some cases the child may introject a very distorted image due to the child's own sensitivity or predisposition to negative introjects. However, the internal model or matrix that is developed becomes the prototype for current relationships. I think this is true for both our human relationships and our relationship with God. For those who have been traumatized (see Chapter 2) it is more difficult to modify this internal matrix, and it may not be easy for any of us. However, I believe corrective relationships can bring about change and adjustment for the majority of us.

Fairbairn wrote of the more positive introjects (internal representations of self and others) in terms of the positive ideal object that embodies the comforting and rewarding aspects of the internal world and the rejecting and exciting introjects that embody the negative aspects. The ideal object is similar to object constancy discussed by Mahler when she describes the ability to comfort and soothe oneself and deal with ambiguity.

> Fundamentally, constancy is our emotional acceptance of the idea that we are neither saints nor demons but whole persons who are capable of ordinary human love and ordinary human hatred. . . .When the good and the bad are split apart, the wholeness of the self fragments and disintegrates. And it becomes impossible to appreciate and respect the wholeness of others. . . . Constancy is also the reconciliation of our everlasting longings for perfection with our down-to-earth daily existence.[12]

At the other end of the spectrum are the rejecting and exciting introjects. The rejecting introject is the need-denying aspect of life and is experienced by the hostile or withholding relationships and experiences of life. In extreme cases it can relate in the person feeling chronically unloved and unwanted. This can be manifested in chronic anger and depression.

The exciting introject is the need-exciting aspect and is developed by the tempting, but unsatisfying aspect of relationships and life. This introject is the result of excessive relationships that promise much but provide little substance. Anticipation and excitement are followed by disappointment. The results can be chronic frustration and emptiness in which one always has a desire, but never finds satisfaction.

Although I see theories such as this as mainly putting language to relationship dynamics, they are helpful in our understanding. They assist us in realizing that many crises in relationships are an outgrowth of prior relationships or are intensified by our prior relationship matrix. Often in my work as a therapist I will have clients who repeatedly get involved with dysfunctional relationships. Some cannot see their pattern, such as repeatedly marrying alcoholics; others have more insight and ask "Why does this keep happening to me?" "Some are attracted only to those who are guaranteed to bring them grief and frustration (rejecting object). The exciting object is personified by the partner who is almost reachable, who tantalizes, but never delivers."[13]

We all gravitate toward the familiar or attempt to recreate it. Often this is true even if it causes us pain. James Framo describes this process well by writing about the hope and desire we have at some deep level to cancel out, replicate, control, master, live through, or heal what could not be settled internally.[14] Napier calls this "displacement reenactment."[15] He writes of how family members carry psychic functions for each other.

Although members of the family of origin may be long gone or reside in a distant city, they continue to live inside a person

as introjects, internal representations. While a marital pair is
establishing an identity as a couple, they are at the same time,
on an unconscious level, recreating certain aspects of their
separate worlds, their early relationships with their parents.
Together, they recapitulate earlier relationships with their parents. Together, they recapitulate earlier conflictual experiences.[16]

Blanck and Blanck wrote of the ways persons get together for
coupling: some come as mature adults, some with minor deficits,
and some with whole chunks of development missing, expecting
their partner to make up for them.[17] Thus it is not difficult to see
how our internal matrix gets played out in degrees of pathology
or dysfunction.

While I have oversimplified object relations theory, it does
provide a way of thinking about relationships and relationship
crisis. It provides a way of working that assists us in seeing how
many of the crises in our relationships and our beliefs are
associated with the context and history of our experience. Many
of these crises do not just appear from nowhere. They have roots
in the distortions and incorrect assumptions of living in this
world. This may be of help in giving us direction as to how to
work on areas in our lives or how to minister to others in crisis.
The next section will present some preventive characteristics that
can help families and relationships provide the kind of nurture
and safety necessary to defend against many crises of our lives.

THE BASIC FAULTS OF RELATIONSHIPS
AND FAMILIES

In this section I will draw heavily from a model of relationships given by Jack and Judith Balswick which is illustrated in
Figure 3.3.[18] Some of the basic faults of relationships and families today are the lack of covenant, grace, empowering, intimacy,

commitment, and balance. These needs in families and relationships leave them on precipitous foundations and subject to the crises that create so much havoc and pain in our lives and our society.

The Theism of Relationships and Families

The Hebrew scriptures have given us a model of relationship from a theistic perspective in the relationship between God and Israel in the Old Testament. God established a covenant or relation or promise to the people of Israel. This relationship between God and Israel has been used to give a theological model for

FIGURE 3.3. A Theological Basis of Family Relationships

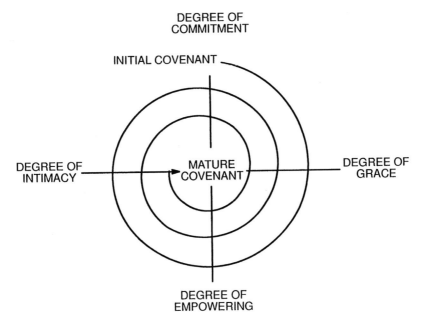

Source: A Theological Basis for Family Relationships by Jack Balswick and Judith Balswick, *Journal of Christianity and Psychology,* 6(6), 1987, p. 39. Used by permission.

parenting that would include loving, caring, responding, disciplining, giving, respecting, knowing, and forgiving.[19] McLean has spelled out the *relational* aspects of covenant as the following:

- People are social and live in community.
- The basic unit of family and thus of covenant is the dyad.
- Persons living in covenant must be willing to forgive and be forgiven by each other.
- Persons living in covenant must accept their bondedness with each other.
- Persons living in covenant will accept law in the form of patterns and order in relationships.
- Persons living in covenant will have a temporal awareness as they carry a memory of the past, live in the present, and anticipate the future.[20]

The Need for Covenant or Commitment: To Love and Be Loved

Balswick and Balswick build a theology of family relationships based upon how God enters and sustains relationships with his people which include the stages of covenant, grace, empowering, and intimacy.[21] These are not strictly linear and are put in sequential stages for descriptive purposes only. They define covenant as having the central point of unconditional commitment. With Biblical examples the case is made that the covenants of God involved unconditional love, but that the potential benefits or blessings in the covenant were conditional. Family covenant relationships can be unilateral (one way) or bilateral (two ways).[22] The parent-child relationship is an example of unilateral unconditional love in that the infant is not capable of reciprocal commitment. "God's ideal for parent-child relationships is for the relationship which begins as an initial (unilateral) covenant to develop into a mature (bilateral) relationship."[23]

This basic fault of a lack of covenant or commitment in relationships and families exists too often today. We are the uncommitted generation. Instead of "when the going gets tough the tough get going" it is "when the going gets tough everyone is gone." That relationships are tough should be a given in our understanding. Not that there has to be constant difficulty, but we must invest and commit for relationships to develop and grow. Covenanting and committing together in love for one another also lays the foundation for grace.

The Need for Grace: To Forgive and Be Forgiven

The second stage in this model is grace. The emphasis is: family relationships are to be lived out of an atmosphere of grace and not law. There will be law in the sense of patterns, order, and responsibility in relationship, but not in terms of demanded perfection. "Grace means that order and regularity are present for the sake of human needs and not the reverse."[24]

In a law-based family there is little room for forgiveness. An extreme example is the family in which there is wife abuse. Typically in such families the wife has to account for every minute of her day. When she is late coming home there is no grace; instead there is accusation and condemnation. There is little room for autonomy or freedom. A rigidity in seeking to conform and please the man is established around the fear of being beaten. Mistakes are not tolerated and may bring the wrath of the abuser. The patterns, rules, and laws of the family no longer serve as a guide or structure—they become prison walls.

Grace-based family life recognizes the need for structure and regulation, but only within the boundaries of promoting organization, growth, and safety. Grace provides for forgiveness when mistakes are made, for beginning again when a wrong turn is made, and for loving support when emotional wounds are experienced. The family can be a haven from the pressures and rejections of day-to-day life in a grace-based approach.

Grace relates very well to the concept of a secure holding environment, which was mentioned in Chapter 2. It is in the atmosphere of security and grace that a person can feel free to explore and risk in such a way as to promote growth and mature development.

Persons can reach for new areas of growth when they feel secure and accepted and know forgiveness is available when they fall short.

The Need for Empowering: To Serve and Be Served

Empowering is another stage and basically means in this context to establish power in the other person. "Empowering is the process of helping the other recognize strengths and potentials within, as well as to encourage and guide the development of these qualities."[25] Relationships, marriages, and families should empower us to grow and develop to our fullest potential.

Empowering was exhibited by Christ in the way he interacted with others. His model was often to treat the marginalized persons of society with utmost respect and acceptance, thus empowering them to find new perspectives of themselves. Instead of using his power in an abusive way, he assisted others in finding their own power and drawing from his. He was willing to walk with others and show them how to find their own way. His statements such as "take up your bed and walk," and "neither do I condemn you; go and sin no more" were tremendously empowering and therefore transforming to those to whom he spoke. Such confidence placed in our family members could revolutionize their lives and give them abilities they have never recognized.

The polarity that we must struggle with in families and relationships that often impacts upon our ability to empower is between autonomy and dependency. This is an issue in couple, parent/child, and other close relationships. How much do we move toward separateness and how much do we move toward togetherness? Especially in parent/child relationships this can be a struggle. I recently had two sets of parents bring their adolescent children in for therapy. In exploring the family dynamics in both of these families, I discovered that a parent in each was actually in subtle and not so subtle ways keeping the adolescents dependent upon them. This approach backfires:

> . . . dependency is a theme which seems to get in the way of the family members empowering each other. In the frailness of our human insecurity we are tempted to keep others dependent upon us, and in so doing find a counterfeit security in having power over them.[26]

Empowering is not a controlling or a protracting of dependency, but an ability to serve others in such a way that they will develop and mature. It also includes the ability to be served by others in such a way that it enhances their own growth as well as your own.

The Need for Intimacy: To Know and Be Known

Lastly, the Balswicks discuss the stage of intimacy, which in the family is to be a process of communicating, sharing, and caring so that members can really know each other. We are created with a need to know and be known—to be in relationship. The Genesis statement is "it is not good for man to be alone." Carl Jung wrote, "The unrelated human being lacks wholeness, for he can achieve wholeness only through the soul, and the soul cannot exist without the other side, which is always found in a 'you.'"[27]

The Judeo-Christian religion is not a "lone ranger" type of life. Instead it is much more of a community-lived experience. Today in the United States we have developed a much more individualistic and isolated religious and personal experience than communal. This has carried over into our relationships and families. We too often relate on a superficial level, which leaves us feeling empty and shallow. Relationships are often used to get our sexual needs met or to connect us with a business or political advantage rather than to truly connect us with each other.

The resulting deficits in our lives are leaving us more susceptible to feelings of inadequacy, low self-esteem, loneliness, and lack of meaning. A spiritual crisis is created where we do not know who we are or where we belong. We sense a deep longing to be in touch with someone at a more profound level, yet this often eludes us and keeps us grasping for something more.

Crowther and Stone define intimacy as "the transcendent self expressing and fulfilling itself in relationship with another."[28] They also discuss how intimacy needs on the spiritual and emotional level are similar to our need for food and water on the physical. Of course, we can survive without intimacy—many do—but what happens to our souls when it is lacking? Wynne and Wynne give a working definition of intimacy as: "a *subjective relational experience* in which the core components are *trusting self-disclosure* to which the response is *communicated empathy*."[29]

The Balswicks draw a parallel for human intimacy from the Christian view of the relationship of God with humans. A theme of the Judeo-Christian scriptures is that God desires to know us and to be known by us.[30] Prayer can provide a means of intimate communication with God. Scriptures such as the Psalms provide a model for intimate self-disclosure and communication with God. The characteristics given above of covenant, commitment, grace, forgiveness, empowerment, and serving provide foundational models for the development of intimacy with God and with each other as family members.

God as a Model for Relationships

The Christian story of God's desire for and pursuit of relationship can be a model for us in relationships of human origin. As can be seen from the above discussion, we can derive a model to promote the characteristics of such things as covenant, grace, empowering, and intimacy from Judeo-Christian redemptive history. Keeping these concepts in balance and perspective can be a means of prevention of some of the crises so characteristic of our age.

Relationships, therefore, can give us glimpses of God and the way God desires to relate to us, but can also reveal the worst kind of evil. For the stability that is preventive against many crises and that sustains us during times of crisis we need a safe "holding environment" where we can reach our fullest potential and where the stressors of life are put into perspective. At their best, our relationships and families can provide this for us. At their worst, our families are the sources of many stressors and crises in our lives.

Even in the best of families, there is no question about the accumulation of stressors being experienced by individuals and families today. The next section deals with a way of conceptualizing this stress.

FAMILY STRESS THEORY

Some of the most helpful conceptual material on families in crisis comes from family stress theory.[31] The earliest work on this was done by Reuben Hill and was called the ABCX family crisis model with the basic outline as follows: "A (the stressor event)—interacting with B (the family's crisis meeting resources)—interacting with C (the definition the family makes of the event)—produce X (the crisis).[32]

This early model was later expanded by others into what is called the Double ABCX Model as shown in Figure 3.4.[33] The Double ABCX Model not only looks at precrisis variables, it adds the important dimension of postcrisis variables and the accumulation of stressors that families can experience. The three areas of importance in the Double ABCX Model are the family member, the family, and the family's community.[34]

All families experience stress (the "a" factor). Some families do well with change and even crisis events while other families may become overstressed or even disintegrate. The extent to which the family is able to cope with events can be determined by several factors including the belief the family has about the event, when the event occurs, and the resources and support the family has available.

When a family is stressed, whether expected or unexpected the family needs to adapt or adjust in some way. The "b" factor defines the family's resources for dealing with the stressor. The "b" factor is part of the coping mechanism for resisting as well as resolving crisis. However, it is not just the resources that mediate the impact of the stressor; the "c" factor or the family's subjective perception of the stressor and the definition it gives to the stressor can be critical. The family's beliefs about the event, their outlook on life, and the way they have met previous crises all influence this factor.

The "x" factor is the amount of change or disruption that all the above factors have caused. Crisis is the point beyond which the family is able to make adjustments and not change. Crisis is the inability to restore stability due to the pressure to change. In some families certain stressors do not reach the crisis stage because they are resolved or resisted and the family stabilizes.

The above basic structure has been expanded to now include postcrisis variables over the life of the family system. These postcrisis variables are: (1) the aA factor or the accumulation of stressors over the family's life which may influence the family's ability to cope, (2) the bB factor which is the combined existing and new resources of the family, (3) the cC factor which includes the stressor, and added stressors, as well as initial and new resources and perceptions of what needs to be done to restore balance, and (4) the xX factor or the family's crisis which includes the initial adaptation or adjustment and postcrisis.

FIGURE 3.4. The Double ABCX Model of Family Stress

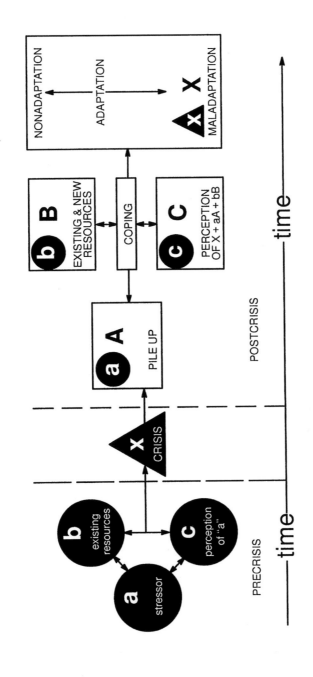

Source: *Advances and Development in Family Stress Theory and Research* by Hamilton McCubbin and Joan Patterson (Editors), 1983, p. 12. Copyright by The Haworth Press, Inc. Used by permission.

This model can be helpful when working with families. It is easy for us to define the reaction of families in terms of our own beliefs about what is normal and from our own experience. Thinking of the family system's current experience with stress and crisis, the timing of transitions it is going through, along with the prior stressor and crises of the family may help us to have more understanding of their adaptation or lack thereof. Caregivers may assist in making family stressors and crises more manageable by encouraging families to find new meaning or purpose in the events of their lives. This may be a time of belief transition (see Chapter 5) for one or more family members or for the family as a whole. Most families initially narrow their focus when under stress and may, therefore, be blinded to options. Caregivers can facilitate exploration of neglected options. Spiritual beliefs can be a source of meaning and strength during crisis and can move the family in new directions. Also, the caregiver or church may be able to help assess the resources of the family and provide needed support structures. Social and spiritual support is of course critical and can be an important factor in the way a family adapts under stress. The family history is important in not only understanding the accumulation of stressors, but also ways the family has been able to endure in the past. Exploring and having families tell stories of past successes in overcoming stressors can assist the family in realizing its strength and having confidence in the present crisis.

Some families have a philosophy that views life as a challenge; they believe difficulties will eventually work out in a positive way and thus are able to treat crisis as opportunity. Some families bear great adversity and appear to adapt well. No family has the same history and composition even if the crisis faced by some families appears to be similar. There are multifactorial determinants of each family's coping ability. Recognizing this we should be wary of comparisons of families with each other and judgmental approaches.

Pastoral caregivers and communities of faith often comprise the bB factor of support for families in crisis.[35] Families can greatly benefit from ministry during such times. It may make the difference between a functional and a dysfunctional adaptation to crisis, including spiritual crisis.

Questions for Discussion/Reflection

1. Do you agree that parents often become the first image a child has of God?
2. What do you believe the Judeo-Christian term "in the image of God" involves? How is this present in humans? absent?
3. What are some of the struggles persons have with relationships and families today? What do you think is going on?
4. What does commitment mean in a relationship or family?
5. What percentage of work, family, and community of faith problems do you think are associated with relationship difficulties? What do we need to learn to improve this?

Chapter 4

The Crisis of Disillusionment
with the Church

One author titled a brief article about the church: "Is the church a hole in the head?" Then he quoted a statement by a friend who had been greatly disappointed by the church, "I need a church like I need poverty or leprosy. You know the greatest hindrance to Christianity is churchism."[1] One of the topics that I have heard most as a minister and as a therapist is the crisis of disillusionment with the church. Many have been hurt, wounded, and emotionally bruised by the church. One survey discovered many have a love/hate relationship with formalized religion. The same survey found a lack of trust in of the church manifested by few respondents stating they would go to persons in their churches during a time of crisis.[2]

Even from leaders loyal to the institution we hear their struggles and concerns as they refer to the church: ". . . we are wasting away like a leukemia victim when the blood transfusions no longer work. . . . Now we are tired, listless, fueled only by the nostalgia of former days, walking with a droop, eyes on the ground, discouraged, putting one foot ahead of the other like a tired old man who remembers, but can no longer perform."[3] Robert McAfee Brown quotes a late medieval manuscript which stated: "The church is something like Noah's ark. If it weren't for the storm outside, you could not stand the smell inside."[4]

In this chapter some of the basic complaints about the church will be explored and how human dynamics complicate church life. These dynamics are often present in the crisis of disillusionment with the church. The concepts of first and second order change will be described and applied to the church. Finally, characteristics that the church needs to exhibit will be given.

IDEALISM AND THE CHURCH

Often we look for a perfect church or we initially think the church is much like the beginning of a lover's relationship and will fulfill our every need. In family therapy we call the period of initial attraction in a relationship "romantic idealization."

Romantic idealization includes the great expectations and "wow" part of a new relationship which blinds us to many flaws. The same often happens in our relationship with the church only more so because of the magical expectations and powerful unconscious fantasies we project upon it. But then comes the let-down. We find the church does not respond as we expected each week or especially during a life crisis. We see a leader in the church involved in dishonest business deals. We begin to see a political process going on in the church which excludes those not of the "old guard." The minister or priest is not as warm and caring as we expected of a person in such a role. Church members are found to bicker over the silliest things. It just does not go as we expected in the church. Sometimes the myths in Table 4.1 set us up for a letdown. Disillusionment and disappointment hit hard and can precipitate a spiritual crisis. This disillusionment may be over theological positions taken or issues of what is proper Christian behavior, but most often I believe it is relationship disappointment at the most basic level.

To those of us who have heard many of the sermons regarding the early church, another contributing problem is that we often have a distorted view of the early church that elevates the unity of that period to unrealistic proportions. One New Testament scholar put it this way:

Unless we are aware of the problems the early church faced concerning its unity, we will inevitably romanticize that period and either give up in despair at the course taken by subsequent developments in the history of the church, or else assume in a naive way that all it takes to recover that lost, original unity is a little goodwill and some pleasant negotiations. . . . Unless we are clearly aware that such a romantic view of an original unity does not stand up under historical scrutiny, all contemporary attempts to achieve unity will be unrealistic about the problems facing the quest.[5]

The early disciples misunderstood the whole purpose of Christ's plan and place in history as they dreamed of an early kingdom. They even bickered among themselves about their status in this new kingdom on the night Christ was betrayed. They tucked their tails and ran when Jesus was arrested. They suffered from jealousy, envy, fits of anger, depression, and all of the maladies we fight in our lives. One was even involved in a shady business deal with those seeking to destroy Christ. So the church has never been lily-white and never will be on this earth.

TABLE 4.1. Ten Crisis-Making Myths About the Church

The myth that:

1. the church is perfect.
2. the church has all the answers.
3. the church has no answers.
4. the church must continue in the same old way.
5. the church must change everything.
6. the church can meet our every need.
7. the church has no cultural and denominational biases.
8. the church doesn't have to answer any of its challenges.
9. theology is the greatest spiritual interest of its members.
10. the church can no longer be relevant.

The Protestant reformers talked about the church "visible" and the church "invisible." The church visible was considered to be all those who were associated with the church and included those who are sincere and those who were there for other purposes. The church invisible was considered to be those who were truly followers of God. Obviously, not all of the church visible is a part of the "true" or invisible church made up of those whose hearts are desirous of God. I am not sure if this is a helpful explanation of some of the problems in the church, but it appears to be comforting to some.

I have always enjoyed the statement attributed to the great preacher of the 1800s, Charles Spurgeon. It is told that a gentleman said to him one day, "I'd become a member of the church if there were not so many hypocrites in it." Spurgeon replied with his usual wit, "Come on in brother; one more won't matter." And that is the bottom line, isn't it? Imperfect sinners will never create a perfect institution even if it is founded by Christ. It has been so from the very beginning and so will it ever be. And what if the church was a perfect institution? Would we really feel comfortable belonging to it? Would it be a place where we could bare our souls and admit our sins? I have had my times of disillusionment with the church, but in my quieter reflective moments the church, frail and frustrating as it is, has been a source of comfort with persons struggling against their own sinfulness as I have myself.

THE CHURCH IS LIKE ANY OTHER HUMAN ORGANIZATION

What should we expect from the church? Is it just like any other human organization? The first answer to this question is "yes." While we hesitate to face this, I think we would be much better off to answer in the affirmative. Yes, the church is often just like any other institution as far as how people interact and human processes go. It has helped me come to accept that the church is a divine/*human* institution. We often do not want to accept that God has chosen to work through the human predicament with all its flaws, sins, selfish aims, and competitions.

The Church and Family Dynamics

Rabbi Edwin Friedman has written about churches or synagogues functioning according to the dynamics of family systems. He describes what he calls "live wires loosely flapping about" in the church which come from unresolved issues of families of church members and the church "family" itself.[6] Thus some religious institutions function as healthier "families" than others. Certainly in some churches members reenact dysfunctions from their families.

Some churches have very rigid boundaries and do not permit easy access. Visitors may immediately feel this when they visit or it may take awhile for a newcomer to encounter the barrier to new ideas and new persons. Just as a closed family system tends to become more dysfunctional, so do closed churches. They become stagnant and have an inbreeding of ideas and beliefs; a type of theological incest develops. In extreme cases:

> A closed system of truth results in closed minds. The faithful are not supposed to—and in most cases dare not—think outside the boundaries of the closed theological system. . . . The Christian life ceases to be a pilgrimage. Instead if offers a security with a certain appeal, but it is too much like the security of the totalitarian state. . . . In the church system, however, the loss of true humanity is worse, because control of the mind is worse than control of the body.[7]

Healthy churches tend to be open and flexible to new ideas and new members. They are able to look more closely at themselves and laugh at themselves. They are less threatened by those who believe differently. They can test the different or new and accept what is good and leave behind the parts that are bad. John Wesley had this attitude when he refused to let differences of opinion divide and made the statement: "If thine heart is as my heart, if thou lovest God and all mankind *[sic],* I ask no more: give me thine hand."[8]

First- and Second-Order Change and the Church

Family systems theorists discuss the terms first- and second-order change.[9] First-order change involves moving things around without really changing the system. For example, a child in a certain family role leaves home and the next child in line assumes this role. A child who has been the scapegoat or black sheep of the family may leave and the next child then becomes the focus of the tension in the family. Or the family might stop fighting about one issue only to place their conflict on another issue. The family system basically remains the same. Second-order change, on the other hand, is a restructuring or higher level change of the family system. The family described above would, instead of passing the role along, change its organization. They would deal with the family tension in a new way. The system would be different.

These concepts have been applied to Christ as change agent as seen in Table 4.2.[10] These authors describe the second-order change that Christ brought. The current theology of the day placed emphasis on keeping the law and seeking salvation by human effort. Christ revealed that salvation did not rest within the individual, but with God. Therefore, change comes from outside. "Christ changes the rules of the system; people are justified, not through their law-keeping, which is more of the same, but by faith in Christ. Common sense solutions (trying to repay for one's own sin) do not work."[11]

TABLE 4.2. Two Systems-Level Interpretations of New Testament Concepts and Events

Concept or Event	Earthly (First-Order Level)	Spiritual (Second-Order Level)
Jesus feeds 5,000	People want more bread	Jesus is the Bread of Life
The Law	More strict adherence to gain salvation	A schoolmaster to point to Christ
Jesus' death	Pharisees plot his death to defeat him, disciples despair	Jesus' death is victory over sin, and death itself
Jesus warns of the leaven of the Pharisees	Apostles discuss their lack of bread	Leaven is false teaching
The Kingdom	Pharisees look for an earthly kingdom	The kingdom is spiritual
Nicodemus and being "born again"	How can a man go back into his mother's womb?	The new birth is spiritual

Source: A Systems View of Jesus as Change Agent by Paul Deschenes and Martha Rogers, *Journal of Psychology and Theology,* 9, 2, 1981, p. 131. Used by permission.

I would like to apply these concepts to churches. Some churches operate on a first-order change mentality. Things basically go on as before; there is more and more of the same. The same theology is repeated over and over. The same people are in leadership over and over. I read of one church that had the same Sunday school superintendent for forty-seven years! It may have been that the person was very good at the position, but I would tend to bet that there was not much new energy coming into the Sunday school with the same person being in the position for so long. The solutions to problems are the ones that have already been tried previously. Not all of this is bad or dysfunctional, but if a church gets locked into this pattern it loses many of its possibilities. In sociology there is a concept called cultural lag which basically states that cultures continue to socialize their members to patterns of behavior long after those patterns have ceased to be relevant to a society's survival. There is a profound cultural lag in many of our churches. This may be an area of disappointment because the church does not speak to one's needs as the person anticipated.

At an organizational level, many of the issues that cause disillusionment for church members occur because the church is stuck in first-order change. Many see the church operating in the same manner as it did generations ago and this no longer reaches them. If they have not been raised in the church, the language used by the church may be incomprehensible. It may not speak to their hearts, nor confront the issues of their lives. The message may have truth, but it is weak wine in old wineskins. Churches need new wine in new wineskins.

Years ago Keith Miller wrote of his frustration with the church and stated he wanted to shout the following: ". . . we are not doing anything which is relevant to anyone's *real* needs—*even our own.* We are just keeping the church machine going because . . . well, *because we don't know anything else to do!*"[12] Often the church is not so much willfully being a "hole in the head;" it simply doesn't know what to do and how to get moving in the right direction. Church members, just as everyone else, have many things pulling at their lives and may not have the energy for working out all the difficulties of the church. However, far too often more energy is spent on keeping things the same than would have to be expended for creative change to occur.

On the other hand, some churches use first-order change, but also incorporate second order change as necessary. They listen to new developments and new needs of individuals and the community. They find new ways to express old truths. They are open to changing the organization of the church if it enhances their mission. They are more interested in people than programs and activities for show or just to keep the machinery running. They are involved in the real world with real people. I believe such a church is described by Kung in Table 4.3.

TABLE 4.3. To What Kind of Church Does the Future Belong?

To what kind of Christian, to what kind of church does the future belong?

Not to a church that is lazy, shallow, indifferent, timid, and weak in its faith;

Not to a church that expects blind obedience and fanatical party loyalty;

Not to a church that is the slave of its own history, always putting on the brakes, suspiciously defensive and yet, in the end, forced into agreement;

Not to a church that is anticritical, practically antiintellectual and dilettantish;

Not to a church that is blind to problems, suspicious of empirical knowledge, yet claiming competent authority for everyone and everything;

Not to a church that is quarrelsome, impatient, and unfair in dialogue;

Not to a church that is closed to the real world.

In short, the future does not belong to a church that is dishonest!

No, the future belongs:

To a church that knows what it does not know;

To a church that relies upon God's grace and wisdom and has in its weakness and ignorance a radical confidence in God;

To a church that is strong in faith, joyous, and certain, yet self-critical;

To a church filled with intellectual desire, spontaneity, animation, and fruitfulness;

To a church that has the courage of initiative, and the courage to take risks;

To a church that is altogether open to the real world.

In short, the future belongs to a thoroughly truthful church.

Source: *Truthfulness: The Future of the Church,* Hans Kung, 1968, pp. 49-50, Reprinted by permission of Sheed and Ward, Inc., 115 E. Armour Blvd., Kansas City, MO 64111.

Of course, second-order change in the church can also create disillusionment with members. Many are threatened by new methods. Those who in their own lives are stuck with more and more of the same do not appreciate change. But sometimes we all need to be shaken out of our ruts. Christianity is a second-order religion and to limit it to a first-order religion destroys its power. When the church becomes the institution of the status quo it loses the creative energy of the spirit. A balance must be created between change and stability, tradition and innovation, ritual and spontaneity.

Biblical Illustrations

This motif of the church as being stuck at a first-order level of change is illustrated by several Biblical stories. An adaptation of the popular parable of the prodigal son is a good example. Suppose the younger son left the church and went off to join in more progressive institutions and partying. He ended up destitute and realized that ultimately the church did have something to offer. He decided to return to the church and sit in the pew and worship. The great love and acceptance of God penetrated his indifference. He is undergoing a second-order change of heart as he has come to recognize his great need. Upon his return to the church he is welcomed by the members who recognize the need for grace in their lives and in the lives of others. They welcomed the "backslider" with open arms and even threw a party celebrating his return. There were some in the church, however, who were not so pleased. They did not see any exceptions to the tried and true way of church organization and activity. These elder brothers were angry and bitter that this backslider was getting all the attention and especially that there was a party going on in the church. They had been faithfully doing the same duties of the church and had not been recognized, so why should this person who has been unfaithful be recognized, even if he had returned? The backslider might bring new ideas into the church from the world. This had never been done before and this new way of doing things was spurned.

Another example is the story of the woman caught in adultery. She is pushed and shoved by the church to Jesus, all eyes are riveted upon her. There is something in the voices of the church members similar to a person fishing who has just made a big catch. As moral watchdogs they have been trained to tear the sinner to pieces. They fully expected Jesus to condemn her to death. They at least were attempting to trap him into this. There was no concern for the agony of the woman. They were committed to a legalist approach and were following what they had been taught. They were stuck in keeping the letter of the law without its spirit and purpose of being helpful to people. Jesus turned their thinking upside down. Rather than condemning her again and repeating the law she broke (which, in this case, would be a first-order approach since it would be more of the same the woman had heard before), he instead showed her true compassion. She left with a heart much more impacted and changed than would have occurred with the treatment of the church members. Second-order change transforms hearts.

Another example involves Jesus and his harsh words to the Pharisees. In Matthew 23 he accused them of not practicing what they preached and putting heavy commands on the people which they themselves did not follow. Jesus condemned their hypocrisy of having their own set of laws and rules but neglecting the most important issues of justice, mercy, and faithfulness. At one point he said to these religious rulers:

> Woe to you, teachers of the law and Pharisees, you hypocrites! You are like whitewashed tombs, which look beautiful on the outside but on the inside are full of dead men's bones and everything unclean. In the same way, on the outside you appear to people as righteous but on the inside you are full of hypocrisy and wickedness.[13]

The Pharisees were moving things around and turning things around without experiencing a second-order change that actually impacted their hearts at a deeper level.

The Church: A Projection of Ourselves

The foregoing material has alluded to parts we may sometimes play in our disillusionment with the church. However, it basically has described ways the church may contribute to the spiritual crises of its members. Briefly, I would like to focus a little more closely on how we may contribute to this problem of disillusionment ourselves. I have already noted that sometimes we place unrealistic expectations upon the church. It may be important for us to examine our own projections that we place on the church. Are the very things that are disappointing us the things that we can condemn and blame when we see them in the church and ignore in ourselves? Unwanted parts of ourselves may be easier to fight if they are out there in the church rather than be seen in ourselves. It is far too easy to expect the church to be totally accepting of us while we are not very accepting of the church. It is not very difficult to be perfectionistic and allow little grace for the church while expecting the church to be gracious to us. It can be a human tendency to want the church to minister to our every need while we do not minister to others with needs in the church.

Paul Tournier, using the metaphor of the need to put down roots and the upheaval of being uprooted in the religious sense, wrote the following.

> Really serious . . . is a rebellion that comes to nothing, a purely negative attitude of revolt, which tosses a person about at the mercy of the most contradictory spiritual influences, without his being able to really commit himself to any. It is in such cases that one can speak of a psychological complex of rootlessness, characterized by an obsessive

and nostalgic search for a spiritual home, together with a tragic inability to adopt one. The sufferer argues endlessly with representation of every kind of religion.[14]

Some who are disillusioned with the church are like this and not able to overcome their own resistance to any attachment to an imperfect institution. These hurting persons may have an especially difficult time overcoming the disappointment they have experienced. We need to reach out and hear their pain and accept their frustration. They are gun (church) shy and afraid of being hurt again.

IS THE CHURCH LIKE ANY OTHER ORGANIZATION? NO!

If we return to the question posed earlier: "Is the church like any other organization?", the second time I think we have to answer No! It is a *divine*/human institution. When the spirit of God moves in the church and the true sense of community exists, the church is different. The danger is that the church will not claim its sense of community and will be bypassed because of this deficit. "There is no future for the situation where people experience the church as an institution but find no community."[15]

The answer, at least from one perspective, is that the church has to claim the presence of community that is so needed in our society today. Writing of the ideal church, Nelson states, "Think of the people concerned about you, ministering to your needs and reaching out to you with such understanding that you can share your intimate burdens and your highest joys."[16] This is the sense of community that should be found in the church.

This sense of community is how persons may experience the spiritual. "Our churches are filled with people who outwardly look contented and at peace but inwardly are crying out for someone to love them . . . just as they are—confused, frustrated, often frightened, guilty, and often unable to communicate even within their own families. . . ."[17] Communities that provide unconditional acceptance and love can be a channel for the spiritual to reach persons. The gospel tells us that God does not establish a relationship with us based upon how well we perform or how much we have it all together and neither should our communities of worship. Romans makes this clear with the statement "welcome one another as Christ has welcomed you. . . ."[18]

> I want you to know that we in the church—if we are really being the church—are like the prodigal's father. We're always there. And when we see you, we run to you. Because we know how difficult it is for you to come in the first place. We know you are hurting and that your mind is all messed up. So we come to you and we reach out to you and we tell you: we love you. We do not put conditions on our love.[19]

IS THE CHURCH LIKE ANY OTHER INSTITUTION? YES AND NO!

The church is a *divine/human* institution. It is a mixed bag of good and bad, spiritual and secular, saint and sinner. There are moments when it is the community of God and when it is a community that has wandered far away from God's will and purpose. The real truth, as we look deeply into the church, is that "we have met the enemy and they is us!" Yet we can also see elements of God reflected in us through the church.

> Where the Church has been identified solely with those who are "at one with God" and therefore at one with the establishment—the forces for persevering the status quo—it has become irrelevant. But where the Church can unashamedly

be made up of a fellowship of those who do not have it made, who are looking for more to life either emotionally, politically, financially, or socially, it speaks a relevant word to man *[sic]* and is true to its New Testament calling.[20]

The Church at Its Best

Many of the measures to prevent disillusionment and crisis with the church and enhance the relevance of the church to our age were described by Jurgen Moltmann. He gives the following important features: (1) *An acceptance of one another:* The acceptance in the New Testament is radical. It is forgiving and rises above prejudice.

> We are no longer individualists but a congregation in which the one accepts the other in the way that one has already been accepted by Christ. . . . Congregation is rather a new kind of living together for human beings that affirms:
>
> - that no one is alone with his or her problems
> - that no one has to conceal his or her disabilities. . .
> - that one bears the other even when it is unpleasant and there is no agreement. . . .[22]

(2) *A messianic lifestyle:* The church should exhibit life in the gospel which has a balance of freedom and responsibility. It will not demand uniformity nor narrow-mindedness, but will call for unity in diversity. (3) *An open fellowship:* The gospel offers an invitation to all. It does not exclude and neither should the church have exclusive circles. The church should not be confined to four walls and known faces. It should maintain the principle of John Wesley when he said, "The world is my parish." (4) *A feast of freedom:* Moltmann calls for more festive, spontaneous, and creative worship. Worship should be a celebration. (5) *An ecumenical church under the cross:* The Lord's Supper becomes the

unifying event for the church. We are invited by ". . .Christ who invites the poor and the guilty to the table of God's Kingdom."[23] (6) *A church of the people:* The church should not be the church of the hierarchy or the elite, it must be of the people and for the people. (7) Finally Moltmann states that the church should be: *A congregation formed "from below."* He quotes a couple seeking genuine relationship who said, "We entered the church as isolated individuals, and we left the same way." He calls for a change in this type of experience of the church. There should be spiritual fellowship and care. The reason for the existence of the church is for the congregation.[24]

Thus the church although beset by the problems of its humanity, provides the possibility for true community and fellowship. As we accept the church's human frailties as being our own, we may be able to get past the rough edges and truly find in the church nourishment for our souls. Ideally the church should provide comfort and community during times of spiritual crisis.

Solutions

What can be done to assist those who are disillusioned with the church? First of all, someone needs to listen them. It would be most powerful if the church could be open enough to hear the pain of its members in this regard without questioning their integrity. There are those who are antagonistic toward the church and have no desire to be connected with it—they want to destroy it. While the church needs to hear what those people are saying, it particularly needs to hear those who desire the church but are disillusioned. A large part of the disillusionment is that the church has not been willing to hear honest criticism. So listening to the pain of the disillusioned without formulating a plan to challenge their thinking is a first step.

Second, the concepts presented above can be helpful. Sometimes persons just need to broaden their focus and truly realize the human element of the church. Assisting them with the integration of the good and bad in the church is important.

Third, giving persons permission to explore various congregations can be a step in their finding a community of faith that meets their needs. We often generalize that all churches are the same but they certainly are not.

Fourth, connecting the intensity of their pain to their family of origin may be appropriate in some cases where the church has become a site for the reenactment of family roles and dysfunctions.

Fifth, the problem may be connected with mistaking religion for spirituality, or mistaking church problems for our own weaknesses. The church may be simply a place to project.

> If we hope for the church to survive, we must learn to think and feel and talk as caring believers who are sincerely interested in understanding and meeting the deepest spiritual and emotional needs of unbelievers.[25]

Questions for Discussion/Reflection

1. What are some of the precipitators of crisis in the church?
2. Do you think many are unfairly idealistic about the church?
3. What human dynamics have you seen played out in the church?
4. Can you give some examples of second-order change that you have witnessed in the church?
5. How can the church best survive in our current society? What adjustments need to be made?

Chapter 5

The Crisis of Belief Transitions

Belief usually does not stand still. It grows and develops, regresses, stagnates, and changes. At one level I envy those persons who have accepted what they have been taught and never questioned or struggled with their belief. I have never been blessed (or cursed—depending upon your perspective) with such an experience. Being more introspective, I ponder and wonder about many things. This certainly doesn't make me any holier, but it does provide plenty of food for thought. Socrates is quoted as saying "the unexamined life is not worth living." Others have said that the "unexamined faith is not worth believing."[1]

Most often our society has not appreciated the extent of crisis that can be the result of belief transitions. Belief transitions may occur gradually with no significant trauma; however, in other instances the upheaval is profound and intensely agonizing: "feelings of anger and resentment, emptiness and despair, sadness and isolation, . . . could be seen in individuals struggling with the loss of previously comforting tenets and community identification."[2]

The lack of sensitivity to the impact of belief transitions may be abating gradually as indicated by the inclusion for the first time in the *Diagnostic and Statistical Manual of Mental Disorders* (DSM-IV) of a diagnostic category called "Religious or Spiritual Problem." Although this category is found under the "V Code" section in the back of the manual and not really recognized as a reimbursable code for insurance purposes, it is a move in the right direction. Acknowledging that many such problems are not mental disorders, the manual states:

This category can be used when the focus of clinical attention is a religious or spiritual problem. Examples include distressing experiences that involve loss or questioning of faith, problems associated with conversion to a new faith, or questioning of other spiritual values which may not necessarily be related to an organized church or religious institution.[3]

In this chapter we will look at the concept of belief transitions and crisis. Thomas Kuhn's paradigm of scientific progress will be used as a foundation from which to develop a belief transitions model. We will briefly consider the maps that have been given by Walter Brueggemann with the Psalms, James Fowler with his stages of faith, James Loder with his concept of radical crisis of belief, and Anne Sutherland with her concept of world-frames.

KUHN'S MODEL FOR SCIENTIFIC TRANSITIONS

Thomas Kuhn gives an interesting analysis of the development and progression of science.[4] The structure he gives for the development and change of science is helpful in thinking about other transitions as well. He discusses six areas that we will use for understanding belief transitions:

1. *Preparadigm phase*—Kuhn points out that science develops by first having many competing schools of thought. Eventually one school wins out and dominates, which moves science to the next phase of paradigm.
2. *Paradigm phase*—During this phase the paradigm is accepted and the assumptions about the paradigm are no longer questioned.
3. *Natural Science*—During this phase research and teaching avenues attempt to fit or force thinking into the conceptual box that accepts the paradigm. Contradictions always exist, but they are ignored, denied, or not perceived.

4. *Anomalies*—Eventually the concepts or thoughts that do not fit into the paradigm become too obvious to ignore and become a challenge to the accepted paradigm. During this period doubt begins to be cast on the paradigm.

5. *Crisis*—The challenges to the paradigm lead to intellectual debate and tension with crisis and conflict following. This leads eventually to a new paradigm which competes with the old one.

6. *New Paradigm*—The new paradigm eventually wins out over the old paradigm, or the old paradigm may win if it has success in handling the crisis or failure of both paradigms to deal with the anomalies.

A Modification of Kuhn's Model in Order to Help Understand Belief Transitions

While no single model can adequately portray the variety of belief transitions, I would like to propose a basic model. I discovered Kuhn's model for scientific change and was surprised with how well it fit some of the transitions in my life (see Chapter 6 which was written before I read Kuhn). With a few modifications it also appears to me to fit well with what I have seen happening in individuals, and in the disciplines I am most familiar with—theology, medicine, and psychotherapy. As a result, Figure 5.1 shows the way I have conceptualized belief transitions. Covey describes paradigms as "maps" and points out how we interpret our world through them, rarely reflecting on their accuracy and often even remaining unaware of them.[5]

Often persons have an open approach to exploring beliefs and integrating them into their lives during the prebelief system phase. As beliefs are considered or assimilated they begin to take on a structure which then evolves into a more formalized system. Usually one belief system will eventually dominate, such as the beliefs of a denomination, although we have many belief systems in life and they do not all revolve around religion. Once the belief

FIGURE 5.1. Belief Transitions

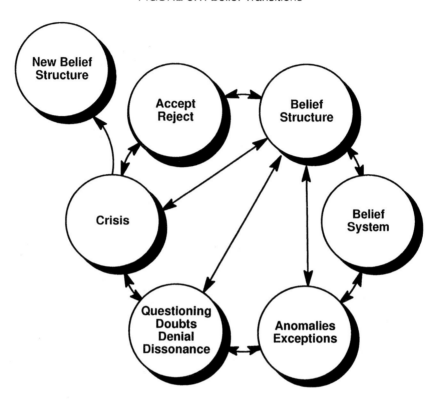

system is accepted it becomes a way of simplifying things by giving a connected framework which accommodates what fits with its model and ignores, minimizes, or denies what does not fit or cannot be answered. Some people appear to never go through the preparadigm phase, and instead accept without question the beliefs of parents, friends, or the church to which they have belonged. For some this is sufficient and comfortable and other viewpoints are barely noticed. Of course, no need for change is felt as long as their paradigm provides meaning and purpose.[6]

A paradigm or belief system is helpful for organizing a mass of material and giving stability. However, it is easy for the structure to become so rigid that it loses flexibility. We can become so fixated in our paradigm that things that do not fit are not even allowed to be considered. William James wrote:

> In all the apperceptive operations of the mind, a certain general law makes itself felt—the law of economy. In admitting a new body of evidence, we instinctively seek to disturb as little as possible our pre-existing stock of ideas. We always try to name a new experience in some way which will assimilate it to what we already know. We hate anything absolutely new, anything without any name, and for which a new name must be forged. . . .[7]

Even with this resistance, eventually many anomalies that challenge a rigid belief structure come forcefully into consciousness. This may be through a crisis or life event that hits us so hard that we have to take note of it. If the anomalies become too obvious or too plentiful, a crisis of belief usually ensues. A belief crisis can precipitate a new growth or a move toward going back to the old belief system with greater intensity. When there is growth it usually brings a new belief system that can incorporate the good of the old system but leaves the part that no longer is helpful and adds the new helpful paradigm.

Others want to throw out the entire old paradigm when it disappoints them. They want to "throw the baby out with the bathwater" so to speak. For some at this point doubt becomes paramount and arrests their spiritual development. Good counsel was given by one author for those in such a position: ". . . perhaps the most important thing to say in dealing with doubt is, live by what you do believe and not by what you question. Unbelief is not a home, no one can live in it. . . . There is no beauty or sanity in a life that hears only the scratch on the record *[or we might say today the glitch in the CD]* and not the music.

Chronic cynicism is a devastating disease."[8] Cognitive dissonance and internal confusion can occur at this phase.

Also there is the route of cycling back to the old belief paradigm if it appears to meet the challenges of new questions or if the person cannot face the shift of change and needs the security of the old paradigm even if it really does not fit for him or her any longer. He/she may find ways to integrate basic changes in the present belief system or may simply go on as if nothing ever challenged it. Some change a belief system gradually over many years. Others have dramatic transformations in beliefs such as the apostle Paul on the road to Damascus. Often persons who are going through such changes struggle with ambivalence. Sometimes a sense of feeling less spiritual occurs if one has moved from a very structured system to one which is less structured. Things are not as clear-cut and defined. One person wrote the following to me during the early days of a transition from one belief system to another:

> I must admit that there are times when I'm not sure what is going on in my head. All I know is that when I think of going back to the "religious experience" of years past, I can't stand the thought. I've found a freedom and a joy that I've never known before, and the more I learn, the better I feel about it. Yet, you can't be raised . . . under the "old school" and not fear, from time to time, that you're not a heretic and a "sign of the end."

From the above discussion, there appear to be at least five major routes that can be taken when persons are confronted by challenges to their beliefs:

1. Development of new beliefs
2. Integration of the old and new beliefs
3. Total rejection of old beliefs
4. Maintaining or adapting the old beliefs
5. Becoming more rigid in the old beliefs

The diagram in Figure 5.1 shows most arrows pointing both directions indicating the push and pull of the cycle and the reciprocal nature of the influences. Belief transitions are rarely if ever linear cause and effect processes.

The Model of the Psalms

Walter Brueggemann gives a structure to the study of the Psalms that fits pretty well with life itself.[9] His schema divides the psalms into three categories: psalms of orientation, psalms of disorientation, and psalms of new orientation. The psalms of orientation articulate coherence, stability, and reliability with chaos and trouble absent. The psalms of disorientation, on the other hand, present the other side of life in the disequilibrium, incoherence, and chaos they describe. Brueggemann also calls these "psalms of darkness" and points out that the amazing thing about Israel was that it did not deny the dark side of religious life as we may seek to do in the church today. This structure of orientation to disorientation to a new orientation reveals a movement from the stable to the chaotic to the transformed. The new orientation is not just a return to the old stability of previous days, but a transformed orientation. Life is like this schema. Belief transitions may be a part of this process and it does not mean that God is absent during the times of crisis or disorientation. God is ever present and often surprises us with new possibilities out of the chaos. This is one reason I think we should read the Psalms often in times of difficulty: they are true to our innermost struggles.

CRISIS CAN BRING BELIEF TRANSITIONS

We have already noted that trauma can bring with it a crisis of belief; as the world of the traumatized is shaken, so is his/her belief structure. Some of the crises that can result in belief transitions and possible spiritual problems are: the loss or questioning of faith, change in denominational membership or conversion to a new religion, and intensification of adherence to beliefs, practices, new religious movements, and cults.[10] While not attempting to be exhaustive I would add: experiencing various forms of loss, experiencing personal illness or illness of someone close, disillusionment with the church, and life-cycle transitions. Often it is crisis or tension that precedes or even precipitates a reformulation of life meaning. The earlier structure must be superseded, broadened, or changed, but not always thrown out when it becomes inadequate.[11]

A Crisis Can Bring Forced Introspection

When our world is shaken by events we do not understand we begin to question our assumptions about life. Often there is an obsessive quality to our questioning and introspection which sticks in our minds like glue. Every way we turn we notice something that reminds us of the crisis in our lives. Movies and songs touch us in more sensitive ways. This can move us toward more reflection and introspection than normally occurs in our lives. As a dog with a bone, when this forced introspection grabs hold it does not want to let go until we are able to get some resolution or stabilization of our belief system.

Crisis Can Bring Cognitive Dissonance

We begin to experience a contradiction between what we have believed and what we are experiencing or between our beliefs and the ways we are beginning to see things. This can be a very troubling experience. It may feel as if all we anchored our lives upon is being pulled out from underneath us. John Rogers notes that many Christians are afraid to face the dissonant part of their belief and states: "rigorous adherence to a faith tradition without regard to their distinct personality and situation in the world may lead to disorientation, frustration, or inappropriate guilt."[12] Cognitive dissonance is the contradiction or conflict that develops between beliefs or between experience and belief. Often what was once a firm belief or doctrine eventually no longer appears to hold up in real life experience. This sets up contradiction and struggle if a person is in touch with him/herself. There will always be contradictions and ambiguities in our belief structures, but these should not become exacerbated to the point whereby they deny the authentic life. When this occurs some give up the beliefs to get some resolution or they may capitulate to those in authority.[13] There might be less extreme reaction and deception if we could seek to address these areas and resolve or at least understand them better. At the least, there needs to be more open discussion in our churches regarding how our ideals are contradicted by our imperfections.

BELIEF TRANSITION CAN BRING CRISIS

Just as a crisis can bring a belief transition, so too can a belief transition bring a crisis. Change in belief does not often come easily. It usually occurs in a time of crisis. On the other hand, belief transition can precipitate a crisis in family, church, community, and nation. The Reformation brought tremendous change and a backlash of reactions throughout Europe. Christ went against the established traditions and was called Beelzebub, the prince of demons.[14]

Some belief transitions are dramatic and are described well by the word conversion. A person may be radically transformed and the evidence is readily seen by all. Other belief transitions are more subtle and may occur as a gradual process over many years. Some transitions radically alter the direction of a person's life; other transitions change a particular view. Just as individual and family psychotherapists have noted that more symptoms occur at critical transitions of the individual or family life cycle, so is it with belief transitions. A person may be more prone to withdrawal and introspection, anxiety, depression, anger, obsessional thinking, and confusion at the time of a belief change. Many belief changes come as a result of the old structure no longer providing adequate answers or satisfying deeper longings for spirituality or fellowship.

The initial result can be very disturbing as people realize that what they have believed is no longer true or no longer works for them. Some find themselves in the position of seeking to simply stay afloat spiritually. Some give up the quest for spiritual or religious fulfillment altogether.

On the other hand, positive emotions such as a feeling of freedom may be present. Such positive emotions are found in the New Testament among those who experienced a release from the condemnation of the law. New energy may be manifested by the excitement of the new beliefs. New associations and friendships are often formed with persons of similar beliefs. A new dedication and commitment is often evident to those accepting a new belief system.

Even religious institutions have not been sensitive enough to the struggle and crisis some individuals experience with belief transitions. Often churches encourage change without supporting the person who makes the change. Often there is little opportunity to verbalize personal struggles with faith within religious institutions. Many churches require blind loyalty or at least outward unquestioning loyalty. As a result, individuals are left to go through honest doubt and searching alone. The pastor or counselor who can allow the verbalizations of such struggles may help smooth transitions so that the changes do not become destructive or extreme.

BELIEF TRANSITIONS: CONTINUITY OR CRISIS?

The Variety of Belief Transitions

The New Testament contains the record of persons experiencing belief transitions or in some cases, belief upheavals, for example, those early Christians who had been of the Jewish faith. With the acceptance of Christianity their belief structure was challenged even though there were many commonalties with Judaism. We find in this record of belief transitions all types of reactions. Some apparently saw Christianity as having continuity with Judaism and made the transition in a less drastic fashion. There were those who accepted the new belief system and became overzealous for the cause. There were some who initially accepted the new belief system and then turned back to their former beliefs. Others sought to have a compromise between Christianity and Judaism.

Belief Transitions As Continuity: Fowler's Stages

James Fowler has attempted to understand belief transitions in the last few decades by developing a framework of stages of faith.[15] Although we will only touch on his model here, it probably contains the most well-known approach to faith development. Fowler delineated six stages of faith:

- *Stage 1: Intuitive-Projective Faith.* This is the child faith that begins at approximately two years of age and continues until about age seven. This stage of faith encompasses a heavy component of fantasy and imagination. It is an elementary level that is based more on fantasy than thinking.
- *Stage 2: Mythic Literal Faith.* This stage normally begins around age six and lasts until around age eleven or twelve. This stage continues to be more of a reflection of the beliefs of others as the child understands them. The child expresses interest in stories, but does not have the capacity to really reflect on their meaning. The stories are perceived literally.
- *Stage 3: Synthetic-Conventional Faith.* This stage usually occurs in adolescence and involves a strong identity with a peer group. A beginning ability to understand deeper meaning is present, but the peer identity usually prohibits true individuality from occurring.

- *Stage 4: Individuative-Reflective Faith.* During this stage a new ability for self-reflection occurs. The individual often doubts or struggles with traditional concepts and beliefs during this stage as is typical in young adulthood.
- *Stage 5: Conjunctive Faith.* This seldom occurs before middle age and involves an integration into an identity beyond the self to others. The individual has the ability to see various perspectives besides one's own beliefs and values. The ability to see many sides of an issue comes with this stage.
- *Stage 6: Universalizing Faith.* Fowler believes only about 2 percent of the population reaches this stage of faith development. He cites Gandhi, Martin Luther King Jr., and Mother Teresa as examples of persons who reached this stage. It involves faith being more than a set of beliefs or even a way of life, for with this stage comes a total commitment to an ultimate cause.

Fowler's schema has been criticized for an elitist quality in that it can appear to have faith dependent upon better education, socialization, and so on.[16] It suggests a hierarchy of beliefs which puts one stage of faith higher than others. Its progression is probably too precise to be truly realistic. I prefer to think of belief transition and belief cycling rather than stages. Fowler's schema is helpful in thinking about various transitions in faith, but the stages do not necessarily mean there is more faith at a particular level. Fowler is careful to state that a person can have a meaningful faith at any stage. A person who is very literal in faith may have a great faith. Children exhibit this for us and Christ said, "Except you come as one of these. . . ."[17] I have known persons with a very literal and (to me) rather limited belief paradigm who nonetheless were spiritual giants who exhibited genuine love in their interactions with others. Even if we use Fowler's stage approach I think we all cycle back through the stages at times in our lives so that we may become more literal in our beliefs at some points even after developing a faith identity of our own.

Belief Transition As Radical Crisis: Loder

James Loder sees more of a "crisis of discontinuity" of development in that he believes most growth occurs during these crisis points between stages rather than in each stage.[18] For him "transformation occurs in alienation, discontinuity, or conflict."[19] Loder writes, "transformation occurs whenever, within a given frame of reference or experience, hidden orders of coherence and meaning emerge to replace or alter the axioms of a given frame of reference and reorder the elements accordingly."[20]

Belief Transitions As Crisis and Process

Rhodes contrasts both Fowler's and Loder's theories. He states that Loder is against any reliance upon natural progress and development as the fundamental basis of transformation. Thus Fowler's stage theory may give more weight to continuity while Loder's theoretical model appears to place more emphasis on the crisis moment. Fowler's work draws a clear connection between creation and redemption in which one does not negate the other; the continuity exists. Rhodes concludes: "I would like to suggest that redemptive transformation is best characterized as having dimensions of both crisis and process."[21] I think this integration and openness to the varied dimensions and experiences of belief change is important for understanding the variety of valid transformations in life.

Worldframes

Anne Sutherland uses the term "worldframes" to describe cognitive structures which are similar to what we have been calling belief systems. She uses a helpful analogy:

Picture a round room, high in a tower, with four windows equally spaced around the wall, each overlooking a view on the horizon. The windows are the same size and height, with a solid space of wall between them. It is possible to walk around the room and look out each window. Many people might find themselves choosing a favorite for any number of reasons. It would also be noticed that some of the view is the same but each has a slightly different perspective than the next one, and is more different from nonadjacent windows.[22]

She then uses this analogy to show how a window that has become familiar is comfortable until it no longer provides meaning, how changing to another window can be troubling to those who are still looking out the former window, and how a view from a new window may appear wrong to persons comfortable with another. Thus she well illustrates beliefs or worldframes and how we tend to confine our view to one "window" or theological stance.

HOW DO WE MINISTER TO THOSE IN BELIEF TRANSITIONS?

Extensive research in the *Faith Development in the Adult Life Cycle Project* found that crisis experiences have a large role in the stimulation of faith development and that most change in faith takes place at life transitions.[23] How can we be sensitive and helpful to persons during these times so that their belief or faith may develop in positive ways? The following suggestions for caregiving during such times summarize the discussions in this chapter.

1. We have to try to look through the other person's "window" and respect ways it may present a view different from our own. This does not mean we have to compromise our view, but we do need to appreciate the other.

2. We need to affirm the faith in the belief of the other person.[24]

3. We need to listen to those who are in pain because their belief systems are no longer working for them and they are on the difficult journey to another belief system or an adaptation of the old one. This can be a lonely journey. A supportive and patient friend or counselor can facilitate the stabilization during this quest.

4. We need to realize and may need to help the person realize that transitions can result in *feelings* of disloyalty or being less dedicated spiritually. Although this may not be the case, the individual may feel very awkward.[25]

5. We most often facilitate a person's growth by providing the support and acceptance needed to lessen anxiety so the person can find the way that is right for him or her. When one's faith is being torn apart, a supporting, nurturing environment may be the only thing that holds it together.[26]

Questions for Discussion/Reflection

1. Do you know persons who have experienced a profound belief transition? How did it appear to differ from persons having a less intense experience?

2. What do you like and dislike about Figure 5.1? How would you diagram it differently?

3. Discuss Fowler's stages of faith.

4. Can you give some examples of belief transitions causing a crisis?

5. Can you give some examples of crisis leading to a belief transition?

Chapter 6

The Crisis of Denominational Identity

This chapter is an overview of my personal crisis of denominational identity. It was a spiritual crisis of horrific magnitude, but it became an opportunity for growth in understanding myself, others, the church, and religious dynamics. It is now one of those events that I would never want to repeat, but one that I would not want to remove from my history.

IDEALISM

It was exciting. It was stimulating. This newfound spiritual belief system blew like fresh rain through spring leaves in the convolutions of my mind. It gave me structure in the midst of my grasping young adulthood. I joined the church, became zealous for the cause, soon packed my bags, and off to seminary I went to prepare for the ministry. For me, the sun rose and set on my new denomination.

Then slowly, gradually, there appeared thread-size cracks, then gaping holes in this belief system I once accepted so readily. At first it was easy to deny the cracks existed—those pointing to the cracks had to be wrong. Slowly the staggering options before me began to confront me like a two-by-four placed forcefully between the eyes. I could continue my theological side-stepping or I could admit to my new understanding. As the theological storm gathered overhead, the castle of theological security I had

---

The original version of this chapter appeared as "The Personal Crisis of Denominational Identity" in *The Pastoral Forum,* Volume 8, No. 1, 1989. Copyright by The Bradley Center, Inc. Used by permission.

built began to deteriorate with increasing rapidity. I was exposed to an increasing crisis of denominational identity. The internal turmoil was terrific.

THE BATTLE

I watched as battle lines were drawn. Labels such as "conservative" and "liberal" made it easier to identify who was on each side. But these labels were also confusing because there was no consensus about what they really meant. Slowly but surely loyalty to the denomination was questioned. If you were in the camp attempting to hang on to the status quo, you were attacked for not understanding the real historical roots of the church. If you advocated change, you were accused of being a radical and not a true member of the church. Shortly, the debate escalated far beyond words to resignations and firings. People who had given their entire lives to the work of the church found themselves ostracized and without church employment.

Theological navel gazing became the favorite pastime. I found myself caught up in hair-splitting discussions and readings. The medieval theologians who debated over how many angels could dance on the head of a pin had nothing on our attention to minutiae. There was a certain enticement, sometimes an addiction, in the pursuit of the answers to the theological controversy. As I now reflect upon it, this was largely unproductive.

THE DECISION

The fact is, I gradually found myself out of harmony with the beliefs of my denomination. My love affair with it kept me hanging on for several years, but the relationship could no longer be sustained. For a number of years, I sought to affirm the things that I could and keep a low profile on the issues that I could not accept or that would create too much controversy. But after awhile this no longer seemed entirely ethical. I watched as my more outspoken friends got fired or were moved to an ecclesiastical Siberia. The spiritual crisis grew inside me until at last I decided to resign and change to another denomination. Later I wrote the following to a friend:

> To put my experience in the form of a metaphor: As you know, I didn't move when a little water got into the ship— when the storm clouds gathered overhead. Many were leaving then and I too was tempted, but I hung on. I didn't leave when the storm hit full force. More left then and I grew more and more frustrated. I attempted to repair where I could even though at times I too wanted to jump. However, when things got back to normal and I realized no preparations were being made for the coming of another storm, that all was back to the same old rock-a-long status quo, and nothing— not even the storm had awakened the captains and most of the sailors, I finally decided it was time to jump ship!

It was a decision made slowly and prayerfully. It was a decision I have never regretted. However, it was a painful decision because many friends and church members felt betrayed and had no understanding of what I was doing. My association with persons from my seminary and my ministerial friends would never be the same again. There was loss involved because of my personal life investment in the denomination. I had to grieve, but the healing has come and I am happy with my decision.

Since these times I have come to realize that what happened to me in my small denomination is only a microcosm of a similar struggle that has occurred and is occurring in many denominations. It has characterized religious groups no matter where one looks in history or where one looks on the face of the globe. In fact, the New Testament rings of controversy. It reminds me of the short poem someone wrote: "To dwell above with saints we love—oh, that will be glory! To dwell below with saints we know—oh, that's another story!" I suppose part of the difficulty has to do with the smorgasbord of personalities we have in our churches, part from our temptation to exclude those who disagree with us due to our own insecurities, part from the way institutions tend to allow the hierarchical assumptions and structures to become so rigid, part from the generalization of theological "expertise," and on and on we could go. Let's face it, none of us and no church has a monopoly on becoming unbalanced.

CONSIDERATIONS FOR THOSE IN A DENOMINATIONAL CRISIS

From my experience and my perspective, I would like to share some reflections on important considerations for those confronted by a personal crisis of denominational identity.

Move Slowly

In the heat of controversy it can be a temptation to react too quickly and later question if one did the right thing. It is best to allow time for processing so as to have as few regrets as possible. Unless conscience is being compromised it is usually best to move slowly. No merit is obtained from being the first casualty in a theological turkey shoot. Be careful not to throw out the baby with the bath water—all religious movements have their share of problems; assess the depth of the conflict and the potential adjustment one can make to it.

Seek Counsel

I found it very helpful to seek out trusted persons of greater experience and discuss the issues with them. Many had the wisdom to give me a deeper insight into the issues at hand. They also helped me distinguish between the trivial and the essential. There was something about this contact with those of more experience that was a stabilizing influence in a sea of uncertainty.

Explore Options

Large institutions normally change slowly if at all. Therefore, it may well be that a denomination has to be left behind for one that is more in harmony with a person's developing beliefs. On the other hand, there may be a place for you that will take you out of the theological battles (at least for awhile) but that will still allow continued personal study and a challenging ministry.

Widen Perspectives

In most theological controversies there are extremes on both sides of the issues. It is easy to narrow our focus in the heat of battle and lose sight of the larger teachings of the gospel. We can lose sight of the monumental teachings such as grace, gospel freedom, and love for God and humankind (even our theological enemies). We can suffer from theological myopia, blind to the larger issues. In 1825 Charles Simeon wrote: "The truth is not in the middle, and not in one extreme, but in both extremes. . ."[1] Not bad counsel to ponder in the midst of extremes. The tendency is to limit our focus to one extreme, believing we have all the "truth." Actually, in such circumstances we need a theological wide-angle lens and a wide-angle heart which takes in even those with whom we disagree.

Allow Grief

There is disappointment when our belief system is challenged, changed, or possibly even collapsed. Shifting something that is or has been so important to us and an integral or intrinsic part of our existence cannot be done without an experience of loss. We may find ourselves with spiritual numbness, confusion, fear, sadness, or anger to name a few reactions. There may be a questioning of more fundamental doctrines in the process. It is important to allow ourselves to work through this rather than stifle the process.

Move On

We cannot maintain the intensity of denominational controversy forever or we will most likely become negative persons. At some point we must stop focusing on the negative and controversial and move on with our lives, even though it may necessitate a change of career position or denomination. The saddest persons I witness in this area are those who have hung on to controversy so long that they are stuck in destructive thought patterns. A life should not be based on negatives. Some controversy can be stimulating and growth producing, but continued feeding on such can leave us spiritual skeletons.

My own experience with a personal crisis of denominational identity was a grueling process, yet it was also a process of my growing spiritual development. I am changed as a result. It has broadened my perspective of the church and of Christian community. I am not as confident as I once was that I have all the doctrinal answers, but there is a certain freedom in realizing that no person and no denomination has all the answers. We are all spiritual pilgrims searching and struggling. No denomination is perfect. However, it is important to belong to a denomination where my spiritual journey is not stifled, but enhanced. The jungle of continual controversy and antagonism has given way to opportunities for my spiritual renewal.

Questions for Discussion/Reflection

1. At what point would you leave a denomination?
2. What are the steps you would go through if you changed?
3. What would be some of the crisis points for you?
4. What do you look for in a denomination to which you would belong?
5. How do you explain why there are so many denominations?

Chapter 7

The Crisis of Extremes

"Life is difficult." So begins the book *The Road Less Traveled* by Scott Peck.[1] This simple sentence has stayed with me ever since I read it years ago. And life truly is difficult at times. It becomes ever more complex in many ways, especially as we make the transition to adulthood. Because of the difficulty involved we seek to simplify life by narrowing our focus and looking at only one aspect of life or living. One author states, "From the moment we first separate yes from no we are polar thinkers."[2] For example, rather than struggle with all the ambiguities and contradictions of living we often focus on one side of a polarity. I call this a "Polarity reaction." This has been described as a defection from growth and as a rigid dualism.[3] I have diagramed a few of the polarities in life in Figure 7.1.

In psychology, splitting is a defense mechanism that prevents the integration of two polarities. We all do this as a defense. However, this becomes more pronounced and primitive in severe mental and personality disorders that often have had trauma as a component of their etiology. Borderline personality disorder is an example. As we have seen in other areas, we learn much about life from those who have experienced the extremes of trauma. It is interesting to note that a treatment strategy for borderline personality disorder has been developed with a basic foundation on the reconciliation of opposites and their synthesis.[4]

Lloyd has given a survey of the ways of interpreting polarities from various cultural contexts such as the works of Plato, Aris-

FIGURE 7.1. Polarities of Life

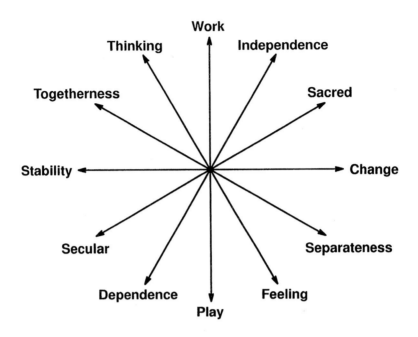

totle, Socrates, Hippocrates, the Chinese (yin/yang) and Durk-heim.[5] I have written elsewhere about the polarities of physicians in training.[6] Brown calls the separation caused by polarity thinking "The Great Fallacy" and states that this is a huge deception particularly when it splits the spiritual from real life.[7] He points out that Judaism has not fallen prey to this deception, but that one influence of the Greek worldview on Christianity was dualism. Another author gives the following critique of our cultural tendencies: "By and large Western culture is a celebration of the illusion that good may exist without evil, light without darkness, and pleasure without pain. . . ."[8]

The suggestion of this chapter is that polarities that become cognitive and behavioral rigidities can precipitate many crises in our lives. They set up false dichotomies which lessen stress initially, but stunt our intellectual, emotional, and spiritual growth. Whether liberal or conservative, we can become unbalanced and focus on one aspect of reality to the neglect of the other side. While the following discussion has some repetition and merging of concepts, hopefully, it will help conceptualize some of the problems with polarity thinking.

SPLITTING POLARITIES GIVES A FALSE ASSURANCE

Whole denominations and movements have been built upon one polarity to the neglect of its opposite. Entire lives have been lived concentrating on one side of a dualism. The following story illustrates this well:

> Once the Devil was walking along with one of his cohorts. They saw a man ahead of them pick up something shiny. "What did he find?" asked the cohort. "A piece of the truth," the Devil replied. "Doesn't that bother you that he found a piece of the truth?" asked the cohort. "No," said the Devil, "I will see to it that he makes a religion out of it."[9]

"We are right and they are wrong" is a common stance taken, sometimes openly, at other times covertly. Therefore, more and more attention is given to the one side or piece of a polarity to prove that it is legitimate and correct. This gives a certain sense of security, but often at a tremendous cost.

Splitting Polarities Results in Lack of Tolerance

Following one line of thinking usually blinds us to the other side and brings forth an intolerance for the contradicting view. To admit or acknowledge any of the opposite side as true begins to crack our security about being right and increases our anxiety that we might even be wrong. We thus compartmentalize our lives to deal with only what can be explained by our belief structure. A conflictual strategy instead of a dialogue based approach is thus set up with others who see things differently. When we make a polarity reaction we try to impose one side and thus develop one way of thinking or acting to support it. This prevents openness to change even in the midst of information that would contradict our polarity reaction.[10]

Splitting Polarities Results in Lack of Challenge

Another way this method of thinking and living impacts is that it removes certain challenges from our lives which results in a lack of growth. We no longer allow ourselves to be challenged by the ambiguities and difficulties of life. While we may have an uneasy feeling of being challenged by the other polarity, we usually keep this as far away from consciousness as possible. This favors maintaining or "opting for the status quo."[11]

Splitting Polarities Results in Lack of Integration

Living on one side of the dichotomy keeps us from hearing and processing the other side. Integration cannot occur. Zalaquett wrote of how polarities are opposite, yet complement and explain each other.[12] When we neglect to truly process and acknowledge polarities we are ignoring a whole area that will result in underdevelopment because the tension coming from integration produces change. "It is the tension between thesis and antithesis forces within the system (positive and negative, good and bad, children and parents, patient and therapist, person and environment, etc.) that produces change."[13] One side seeks to be not only dominant, but to become absolute in most polarity reactions.[14]

Splitting Polarities Results in Lack of Flexibility

Splitting results from rigidity and results in rigidity. We need to be flexible enough to move along a polarity continuum as needed and indicated. Otherwise we will view life and conflicts as inflexible categories of good/bad, white/black, or either/or. Our options and possibilities thus become narrow with tunnel vision. Polarities can be, by their nature, inflexible.

INTEGRATION OF POLARITIES GIVES BETTER BALANCE

Integration of life's polarities moves us toward interconnection and wholeness of life, assists us in recognizing that reality is composed of opposing forces and tension, and directs us to the concept that change is continuous since synthesis of polarities results in still new dichotomies.[15] As we struggle with integration we do not have to force life and thinking to fit a particular mode. We can better live with tensions, contradictions, and ambiguities.

Integration Results in Emotional Processing

Living with polarities can assist us in accepting the contradictions within ourselves by normalizing them. We can, therefore, better acknowledge our hate as well as our love, our selfishness as well as our altruism, and our evil as well as our good. We can better embrace our "shadow side" as Carl Jung called it, rather than denying its existence or projecting it to others. This can result in dealing with our conflicting emotions about ourselves and others. Processing can occur when we listen to the conflicts inside of ourselves.

Integration Results in Motivational Enhancement

Synthesis of opposing forces or thoughts is a means of growth and is motivationally enhancing since it brings us to a new understanding. Heath has written that "if you wish to provoke a person to become more aware, learn how to reflect, think freshly, then disrupt his usual patterns by forcing him into situations that create contrasts, confrontations, and challenges."[16] Zalaquett writes of the withdrawal of negative energy that comes from polarity splitting and states that this takes away motivation and makes life duller.[17]

Integration Results in Interactional Balancing

Integration of polarities makes us less eager to propose we have the final answer and more open to the possibility of hearing the beliefs of others. Integration gives us a greater appreciation for the diversity of understandings and interpretations in life and belief. The resulting willingness to be more inclusive opens us to being taught the limitations of the aspects of life we might be denying or ignoring. This does not mean we do not argue and have firm convictions, but that in the midst of our convictions we can continue to hear what opposing persons are stating. None of us do this perfectly, but an integrative approach to polarities assists us in being less relationally dogmatic.

Accepting both sides of a polarity provides complementary information so that integration can occur.[18] It also assists us in moving back and forth as needed, depending upon the situation:

> . . . every Christian community . . . needs a conservative like James and a progressive like Paul. The church must learn to live in the tension between the old and the new, between the vision and the revision, form and reform. We can't travel very far in a car that only has a brake, and who would risk driving in one that only had an accelerator? There are times in any journey when a motorist needs both to survive![19]

Integration Results in Personal Regulation

Tritt states that when we embrace the many polarities of experience we gain a more confident sense of self.[20] A psychologically healthy individual has many integrated and interdependent parts and polarities and is better able to accept who he or she is.[21] This results in greater personal regulation as emotions and feelings are acknowledged and dealt with rather than pushed down and denied. It is no small matter that within churches where sexual issues are denied or overly controlled, many end up in compromising sexual situations. Sometimes when a person attempts to impose one dimension over another, more subtle power is given to the repressed polarity.[22] "When a person is stuck at the impasse of his own opposing forces, he is at war with himself."[23]

> By allowing expression and interaction of each of these internal parts, the client also achieves a greater closeness among them, increasing his or her inner communication. By recognizing and accepting those parts alienated from him- or herself, the client rebounds with energy, capacity and alternatives of behavior, and the positive functions of each of these parts.[24]

POLARITIES IN THE CHRISTIAN LIFE

Snodgrass with wise insight stated the following about polarities in the Christian faith:

> Tension permeates our faith. Every truth that we know is balanced by another truth that seems to be moving in the opposite direction. . . . Our faith is lived out between two or more competing truths, neither of which may be relinquished. We live between truths. . . . We do not like complexity and tension. In fact, in order to keep life simple we will suppress those things that hint at complexities. We accept partial truths, stereotypes, and generalizations, even if they do not fit the facts. . . . Our attempts to make life and faith simple derives from our need to find some handle by which to control the complexity around us.[25]

Some of the polarities in the Christian life are seen in Figure 7.2. Several of these are discussed by Snodgrass and are familiar once we pause and consider them.

An illustration is helpful in thinking about tension or polarities in the Christian life:

> Tension in the Christian life is not like a tightrope where we must fear falling off either side. There would be no peace in that. A more appropriate image is that of a stringed instrument. Properly attached at the two right places, the instrument can be played. If a string is left too loose, music cannot be produced. If it is stretched too tightly, the string will break.[26]

There are polarities in the Christian life that must be kept in proper tension, but this does not have to be destructive tension. It can be creative as the illustration above so concisely reveals. We must be willing to face the tension if we are to live the Christian calling:

> Especially in our Western culture with its tendency to emphasize the rational and the organized, we need to beware, even in our life with God and with others, of setting up dichotomies that can ultimately force choices damaging to reality, truth, and life—and to the very values in which we wish to grow.[27]

This does challenge any simplistic notion about the Christian life. Life by the way of the cross is not easy and it does move us to deal with the complexity of the life.[28] However, what is challenging is often most rewarding and fulfilling, and this certainly is true of the walk with Christ and the resulting inner peace this brings.

FIGURE 7.2. Christian Life Polarities

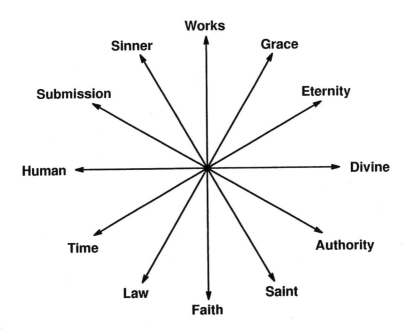

Helping Those at Extremes

One role that I believe is vitally important for a caregiver be it a pastor, counselor, or friend, is helping people see their neglected polarities. As mentioned at the beginning of this chapter, under stress it is very easy for us to lock on to polarity thinking. As Zalaquett has written in a little different context, by a caring confrontation of neglected parts of a polarity, persons can be helped to:

1. contact the fragmented or unknown parts;
2. admit and accept them;
3. reclaim them;
4. integrate them; and
5. convert him- or herself into a whole.[29]

Snodgrass gives these guidelines for assisting with polarity thinking: First of all, we need to practice holistic thinking which begins by recognizing our own incompleteness and being open to persons of differing perspectives. Holistic thinking will help us ask what are the limitations of statements and opinions. Second, we must allow for unity and diversity within the church. The recognition of our incompleteness will require both unity and diversity as we seek to gain the perspective of those who are different from us. Snodgrass cautions that unity is not uniformity and diversity is not division. A third guideline is to accept our humanity. To be human is to have to deal with polarities, tension, and incompleteness. The authentic life has to accept these facts.[30]

So the oscillation and polarity characteristics of life are important struggles we should not avoid. We must deal with complexity if we are to live in reality.

> The words "What God has united let no man put asunder" apply to more than marriage. For, as we have seen, "putting asunder" or away from the psyche any aspect of reality— inner or outer—brings its own inbuilt penalty to human life.[31]

Questions for Discussion/Reflection

1. Are there particular times in life when a person is more likely to go to an extreme? If so, when?
2. Can you give examples of movements or organizations that you feel are based on one side of a polarity?
3. What are your own struggles with "polarity reactions?"
4. Are there any preventive measures one can take to avoid this problem of extremes?
5. What experiences have you had seeking to counsel persons who you felt were being extremist?

Chapter 8

The Crisis of Loss

I write these words after returning yesterday from visiting the relatives of my wife's thirty-year-old cousin, Sandra, who died instantly in a head-on auto and logging truck accident two days prior to our visit. We visited the grieving husband in his home. It was a surreal experience as I walked into the home and saw the pictures on the mantle and items in the house just as Sandra had left them on the day she went to work not knowing she would never return. The house had her touch in the decorating, her love for animals exhibited by the cats running around inside and outside the house, and her clothes still hanging in the laundry room. I wondered how disturbed she would have been by the mud being tracked into her home as visitors came and left.

Her husband had left the funeral home because he stated his wife's presence was not there—so he came home where he felt close to her. He had lost the love of his life, and along with her went the dreams they had of the future, of having children, of growing old together. He was seeking to make sense of it all in his shock. "There must be a purpose." Another family member spoke of her anger and how it did not make sense that someone so good had died so young. She said it almost made her angry at God. The church had brought food. The pastor had comforted as best he could in the situation. Friends and relatives came to show support. But their world was shattered and will never be the same.

When there is loss it penetrates our being like a knife separates the skin. It lays our emotional being open to the raw pain of precious parts of life or relationships being severed. It brings crisis of several dimensions, including spiritual crisis. One person of faith struggling with the tragic loss of his son stated:

> . . . Elements of the gospel which I had always thought would console did not. . . . There is a hole in the world now. In the place where he once was, there's now nothing. The world is emptier. My son is gone. Only a hole remains, a void, a gap, never to be filled. . . . My wound is my unanswered question."[1]

Eibner comments about this father ". . . the unexpected and traumatic death of his son interrupts the flow of his life, challenges the assumptions he lives by, and raises fundamental questions about his whole frame of reference."[2] His loss eventually led him to a deeper faith, but his statements did not indicate a lack of faith. They are the statements of a real person who has a real faith living in the real world with the trauma of loss. This father allowed himself to honestly wrestle with his loss and this moved him eventually to a deeper level of faith.

This chapter will explore the crisis of loss as it relates to death, although much of what will be stated could also apply to other losses such as divorce or loss of relationship, job loss, and the loss of a belief system. Like a light bulb that crashes upon a cement floor, such losses can shatter our life meaning. At such times many ask, "What is the purpose and meaning?" and "Why is life worth living?"

THE DISRUPTION AS THE RESULT OF DEATH

Indicators of More Complicated Bereavement

At the beginning of our discussion on loss as a result of death it should be noted that certain persons may be at greater risk of a more serious form of bereavement. While there is by no means a clear differentiation between those going through normal bereavement and those who are more susceptible to pathological bereavement, especially in the early months, some risk factors may be considered. Those who are confronted by sudden death, those who have inadequate support systems or are living alone, have substance abuse problems, and preexisting psychiatric or medical problems certainly need to be monitored closely.[3]

Some of the symptoms of an unresolved grief reaction can be clinical depression lasting more than one and one half years after the loss, prolonged isolation, emotional numbing, continuing compulsive overactivity without a sense of loss, profound identification with the deceased, and extreme and persistent anger. Bowlby points out that much of the anxiety, depression, and personality disturbance seen in clinical practice may actually be the result of disordered mourning.[4] While most persons will be doing much better a year or so after a loss, a certain void can be felt for the rest of the person's life. "When someone we love dies, a voice inside us tells us our lives are forever altered."[5] Losses from the past may be resurrected when confronted with additional losses later in life.

Cosby and Jose list three dysfunctional ways of dealing with loss: avoidance involving busyness that keeps a person in denial; obliteration or acting as though the deceased never existed, which may involve disposing of all personal effects of the deceased; and idolization that puts the deceased on a plane far above what existed during his or her life.[6] Idolization often occurs to some extent, but can create havoc in the grief process and family life when carried to an extreme in which the deceased is seen as having been perfect.

Ways of Considering the Bereavement Process

The stages of death and dying according to Dr. Elizabeth Kübler Ross are now well known. They include denial, fear, anger, bargaining, and acceptance.[7] These have been adapted to also include the stages of grief, which often include stages such as numbness and disorganization. A better term than stages of grief might be "reactions of grief" since these should not be seen as a one, two, three linear progression, or even as totally separate. Instead they are recursive in nature, often with overlapping emotions. Agitation, guilt, depression, despair, loss of identity, and other characteristics could also be added for many going through the dying process. Reisz states that sometimes these stages are discussed in such as way as to imply that a person has to achieve a certain competence as if there is only one correct way to grieve.[8] However, we must be careful to recognize the differences in each person and situation. Reisz goes on to describe how the stages of death can be correlated with Paul Tillich's four principles of the new being in process: awareness, freedom, relatedness, and transcendence. While these are applied by Reisz to the dying person, they could also be applied to the grieving person.

Awareness, freedom, relatedness, and transcendence can all be compromised during periods of intense loss. Despair, fear, anger, and other emotions, or, conversely, the shutting down of emotions, can block meaning and purpose during such times. It is difficult to be aware and in tune with self or others and experience the freedom that comes from feeling some ability to affect our world rather than be totally affected by it. Relatedness can be eclipsed by feelings of abandonment, and transcendence may be muted in such a manner as to limit our ability to be in touch with God. During loss it may be difficult to obtain any internal comfort or peace.

In his theory of attachment, Bowlby has described four phases of mourning which also should be conceptualized as fluctuating and recursive in nature such as those mentioned above: numbing, yearning, searching, disorganization and despair, and reorganization.[9] Numbing includes disbelief; searching includes yearning and pining for the lost persons as well as restlessness; disorganization often includes depression and the realization that the search is useless; and recovery involves a revised sense of self.[10]

Attachment and object relations theorists have pointed us to the profound need for relationship that exists among humans. When relationships end there is a reorganization of the self that occurs at its deepest level. This is the reason such an emptiness and sense of loss is felt among those who have experienced the death or loss of a close relationship. I have worked with many persons who question themselves about the difficulty in moving on after the death of a loved one. In some cases, they are surprised that they just cannot "get it together" after several months have passed. However, in close relationships we share various internalized collusive aspects of our personalities, so the loss of a relationship is in reality a loss of important parts of ourselves.

The Family and Grief

It is important to think not only of individuals experiencing grief, but also of the family system. Individual members of the same family may have very different responses to loss. This may be based upon their various roles and collusive connections to the deceased. It may also simply be that the family members are going through grief in differing ways or stages.

The family as a whole may be impacted in a very different way based upon the stage of the family life cycle and the role the person played in the family. A family may have been at the breaking point when the loss occurred and the addition of one more stressor may make it almost impossible for the family to get back on track. The family identity may take some time to reestablish. Resources such as finances, support, extended family, and involvement with professionals may also impact the way the family survives the trauma of loss. Although beyond the scope of this book, cultural and historical aspects can certainly influence family as well as individual approaches to and definitions of grief and loss.

RESPONDING TO THOSE WITH LOSS

Needs of Those with Loss

The Robert Wood Johnson Foundation did an eight-year, twenty-eight million dollar study of how hospitals treat persons in the last days of their lives.[11] Among other things, the study asked if the wishes of patients and families were being respected. Amazingly the study found that the wishes of patients were largely ignored and that there appeared to be a conspiracy of silence about death and dying. If professional personnel in hospitals where death is a continual reality cannot discuss death and issues related to death and grief, how much worse this "conspiracy of silence" must be in the general population. And what does this mean to those who are grieving? Where do they discuss their losses? I have had many counseling clients tell me of initial responses of support, but abandonment by others later in their grief. "People don't want to talk about it. They think I should be over it by now." These are statements I have heard all too often.

Assessment and Acknowledgment
of the Spiritual Components of Grief

> The spiritual guide needs to hear clearly the bereaved person's experience from the person's own perspective and listen carefully to the spiritual components of that experience. Does God feel close, distant, or absent? What image of God is the person working with? Does the bereaved person feel anger or resentment that is directed at God? Does the bereaved person bear a burden of guilt? How are the dynamics of fear and trust present in the person's experience? How is prayer functioning in the person's life? How is the bereaved interacting with significant others and with their faith community? Are they tending toward isolation or reaching out? How is the death/resurrection dynamic at work in this person?[12]

The Ministry of Presence

In keeping with the emphasis I have placed in this book on the importance of relationships, it is important here to write of the ministry of "presence." Martin Buber wrote of the height of a person's relation with another as "making present" which he describes as:

> . . . that I imagine to myself what another man is at this very moment wishing, feeling, perceiving, thinking, and not in a detached comment but in his very reality, that is as a living process in this man.[13]

Presence has to do with availability and has an incarnational aspect as when God is with us. It is entering a person's world and being a part of that world, paralleling Christ being in this world. It is much more than just being physical presence. It has profound emotional and spiritual components. It may or may not involve communicating with the use of words. Sometimes, in fact, words can block the ministry of presence and be a way of distancing from the person. When one is truly with another in presence, words may not be necessary.

The ministry of presence is the tender, yet powerful care so often lacking in the rooms of those dying. It is also absent from many of those who are grieving over loss. In loss the comforting inner core is shaken so badly that even very secure and stable persons sometimes have an inability to soothe and comfort themselves. The ministry of presence can be one way of bringing comfort from the outside.

To use Christian metaphors again: loss is what Adam and Eve experienced at the fall and what Hell is truly like. It can bring feelings of utter separation and abandonment. It is the person feeling as though he or she has been cast outside, "into the darkness, where there will be weeping and gnashing of teeth."[14] There is coldness.

> Winter is a season of the heart as much as it is a season in the weather . . . Near the equator, winter is unfelt. As for the heart however, where can one escape the chill? When death comes, when absence creates pain—then anyone can anticipate the season of cold. . . .[15]

The incarnational presence of another goes into that outer darkness and coldness and stays there with the person. I believe this begins to bring healing even if it is not immediately evident.

The "Why?" Questions

The "why" questions during loss are difficult. Howard Stone warns against attempting to provide answers prematurely without really listening and forming a relationship with the person.[16] He also gives the important point that often "why" is not a request for a theological answer, or any other answer for that matter, but a way for a person to express pain or a combination of both a cry for an answer and an expression of pain. He states:

> Many "whys" are actually poetic questions. They are a symbolic way in which the depth of one's misery is expressed. Indeed, for many it is easier to ask "Why did God do this?" than to say "I have had an immense loss, and I am feeling utterly devastated by it." . . . A helpful way to determine whether the "why" is poetic or literal is tentatively to assume that clients are really saying they are emotionally hurt, and respond first to that. The response to "How could God let this happen to me?" may be something like, "John's death is really a great loss for you."[17]

He states that if the client answers "yes, but" it may be that he or she truly wants an answer to the question. Far too often, as Stone also states, persons in pain get answers that are very destructive to their emotional healing. The best answers are not the ones in which a counselor waxes eloquent in theological jargon, but the ones in which a dialogue occurs based upon where the person is and how he or she may have believed. The individual may be in a belief transition based upon the loss, but normally does not need a radical change at the time of impact of the loss.

Robert Beckman notes some of the fears physicians have in giving bad news to patients.[18] Most of these can be related to fears we have about ministering to persons during times of loss: Fear of the unknown and untaught, fear of unleashing a reaction, fear of expressing emotion, fear of not knowing all the answers, and the personal fear of illness and death. Although particularly relevant in the case of physicians, these are fears other caregivers have at some level in various ways. These fears often include the "why" questions of the grieving person as well as of the care-taker.

Mediating Factors in Bereavement

Faith can be a special resource for grieving individuals. It may provide the anchor to keep them from being completely swallowed in a sea of despair. I like the emphasis in the following:

> Persons who in one way or another find the way through the tight place of anguish begin to find an integrity in living toward death that overpowers both the wish to deny and the anger of loss. In the most profound sense such persons become open to the future of both their life and their death. Their faith takes on the quality of eschatological trust.[19]

Religion can certainly be a mediating factor in dealing with death and loss. Often religion at its best can: (1) provide meaning to loss and a way of integrating it into the totality of life, (2) provide a way of coping through the use of rituals, (3) provide a belief system that assists with the transition from life to death and beyond, and (4) provide a way for those who lose their loved ones to deal with and, hopefully, integrate suffering and death into their lives.[20]

> In order to be at peace, it is necessary to feel a sense of history—that you are both part of what has come before and part of what is yet to come. Being thus surrounded, you are not alone; and the sense of urgency that pervades the present is put in perspective: Do not frivolously use the time that is yours to spend. Cherish it, that each day may bring forth new growth, insight, and awareness. Never allow a day to pass that did not add to what was understood before. Let each day be a stone in the path of growth. Do not rest until what was intended has been done. But remember—go as slowly as is necessary in order to sustain a steady pace; do not expand energy in waste. Finally, do not allow the illusory urgencies of the immediate to distract you from your vision of the eternal. . . .[21]

Questions for Discussion/Reflection

1. Do you think all loss is similar? Why or why not?
2. Does the church assist in accepting death and loss?
3. What are some of the destructive words people say to those who are grieving?
4. What are some of the constructive and helpful words to say to those who are grieving?
5. Can you describe the "ministry of presence?" Have you experienced it?

Chapter 9

The Crisis of Physical Illness

When a person sneezes and you say "God bless you," you are following a heritage of invoking the gods to ward off evil spirits. You are connecting the physical with the spiritual. Historically, in many cultures the spiritual leader has also performed the role of physical healer. While there was an influence in early Christianity that saw the body as evil and the soul as good, we are beginning to see that such a view and a separation are not valid. Maybe we are returning to, in some respect, our Judeo-Christian heritage which originally saw physical health as important. This fact is exhibited by the numerous health laws for the Jewish people. Christ apparently spent a good deal of his time addressing physical concerns of people according to the percentage of the New Testament given to this topic. Salvation in the New Testament was much more holistic than Western belief has incorporated.

Science and the Enlightenment have glorified reason and rational thinking to the neglect of the mystic and spiritual. This has influenced medicine and Western thinking. In fact, the church of the Middle Ages encouraged this by allowing dissection of the body, but forbidding medicine to deal with issues of the spirit. This is beginning to change. There is a growing movement in medicine to address the spiritual. Hopefully, spiritual and physical will be recognized more and more as interdependent.

BIOPSYCHOSOCIAL EXISTENTIAL EXPERIENCES

Even though I worked as a parish minister for several years and went on countless clergy hospital visits, I never understood

106 SPIRITUAL CRISIS: SURVIVING TRAUMA TO THE SOUL

the crisis impact of illness until I began working in a medical setting. Day after day of observing sick persons and the limitations and disruptions imposed by their conditions has made me much more aware of the off-the-Richter-Scale magnitude with which illness can shake a life and a family.

Another event that opened my eyes to the impact of illness was our daughter's sickness when she was fourteen months old. She had an infection around her left eye (periorbital cellulitis) which the physician felt had developed into meningitis. The result was that we almost lost our child. Briefly, I would like to share three areas that have become prominent to me since this experience.

First of all, there was my reaction as a parent and family member of the patient, my daughter. There was disbelief. This could not be happening to my precious daughter. She would be okay. This was quickly penetrated by the reality that her infection could have already spread to the brain and she could be disabled or die. Then there was the disorientation. I seemed to be living in a fog; I could not focus on anything. I saw things, but did not really see them. I caught myself not hearing what people said to me.

At first I did not want to talk to anyone about what was happening. Then I wanted someone to talk to and began calling some of my friends to tell my daughter's story (and thus my own). It helped tremendously just to tell the story to others. Of all people, as a therapist, I should have known that. And I did, but it took a while to get past my denial and to realize my need for support. If the caretakers of our daughter could have simply mentioned some of the reactions my wife and I might have to our daughter's illness, I believe it would have assisted us tremendously in normalizing our experience and dealing with it.

Second, there was the reaction and interaction of the health professionals with my daughter. The physicians we used were personable and caring individuals. I was amazed at how important this became for me. To see one physician, in particular, who was so loving and caring toward our daughter was comforting to us in our anxiety about her. We knew this physician cared about what she was feeling and experiencing. His empathy was a powerful force in providing support to our emotional selves. He entered our world with it. I was surprised by how vulnerable I felt and how much a caring nurse or physician shouldered me.

The other area of this experience that impressed me was the interaction of the health care workers with my wife and me, the family members of the patient. They were kind and courteous. They did a good job of keeping us informed of the status of our daughter and the results of lab work. However, I am aware that none of them asked any questions about how we were doing as parents as we witnessed our daughter's illness. Not that we expected them to focus on us, but a brief exchange about our feelings would have been a very healing experience for us, I believe. The health care workers addressed the facts of the disease process well, yet the emotional and spiritual components we experienced as family members were overlooked. I am sure that I have done the same in the past as I visited patients and their relatives even as a clergyperson. However, my experience with my little daughter has carved the importance of the psychosocial, emotional, and spiritual aspects of life into my being in such a way that I am now a true believer in an integrated model of care.[1]

HEALTH BELIEFS AND ILLNESS

For the most part modern medicine has primarily focused on the disease of the patient. It has taken a view of the body as a machine and has, therefore, reduced the physician's role to a mechanical troubleshooter. This view is gradually changing in medicine and more attention is being given to the patient's experience of illness. Some of the important aspects of assessing sickness are: What does illness mean to the patient? What questions does it raise for the patient? What explanations does the patient have for the illness? What feelings does the patient associate with the illness? What are spiritual components of the illness experience which need to be addressed?

Beliefs about health and illness have a wide variation even in our culture. Many times we are taught health beliefs in our families without even realizing it. Often there is a "health expert" in the family. In our society this has often been a female role. But think for a moment about what you were taught about maintaining health and the causes of disease. Some of us learned never to see a physician unless we were almost on our deathbed. Others were taught to go the doctor for the slightest ailment. Some have been taught disease results from disobedience to God's laws. Spiritual healing has been practiced in some of our families instead of going to the medical doctor. We often use the phrase "in sickness and in health" in our marriage vows. So there are family, cultural, and societal beliefs about health and illness.

Arthur Kleinman, a medical anthropologist, has used the term "explanatory model" to refer to the person's interpretive framework or meaning system associated with health and illness.[2] Pastoral counselors, physicians, and other professionals need to understand how the sick person explains his or her illness in order to adequately minister to the suffering person. Rolland has stated that Kleinman's explanatory model concept can be understood as the person's or family's belief system that acts as translator between the disease and what the individual or family experiences.[3] For example, a person who explains illness as punishment from God may have a much different struggle with illness than one who sees illness as an attack of Satan upon them for their loyalty to God. One of the problems has been that professionals who focus only on the disease may miss the meaning the disease has for the individual or family and thereby miss the opportunity to provide the kind of support needed. Professionals need to consider the contributions to the illness experience as illustrated in Figure 9.1.

FIGURE 9.1. Contributions to the Illness Experience

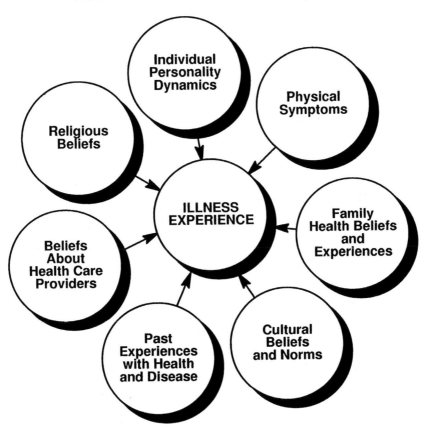

Caregivers need to ascertain what the person is experiencing and feeling in order to stay connected to his or her emotional and spiritual pain. Acknowledging and understanding a person's belief system in regard to illness can be a healing factor in his or her life.[4] Missing these dynamics can leave the person cut off from the ministry one is seeking to provide.

Kluckhohn gives five orientations to assess belief systems. These orientations are the way that some sense is made out of crisis and how coping styles are developed:

1. What do they believe about human nature? Is it seen as good, evil, or mixed? Is it seen as capable of changing or is it set for life? For example, belief in human nature as basically good may lessen guilt.
2. What is their temporal orientation? Is the emphasis on the past, present, or the future? Focus on the past, for example, will give more weight to intergenerational issues and influences from past generations.
3. Is their orientation toward being, being-in-becoming, or doing? In Western culture the emphasis is on performing and doing. Therefore, the loss of ability due to a disability may be more profound in some ways. On the other hand, a doing orientation may help promote activity toward recovery as far as it is possible.
4. What do they believe about the relationship between humans and nature? Do they believe in the subjugation to nature, harmony with nature, or the mastery of nature? These are often related to locus of control and how much a person believes he or she can effect change.
5. What is their preferred relationship between humans? This has to do with orientations toward autonomy and individualism or commitment to the group or family. This can be important in terms of the amount of cohesion or the amount of dependence a person is able to tolerate.[5]

Assessing such beliefs can be of great benefit and can assist in creating a parallel process of agendas between the professional and the person being helped. Otherwise, conflicting agendas may hamper or even halt the ability to communicate and understand.

THE CRISIS OF CHRONIC ILLNESS

Most of us have experienced an intestinal virus or the flu at least once in our life. Remember hugging the toilet bowl as you actually thought your insides were coming apart and you simply wanted to die? During such times we may want to implement the words from the friends of Job: "Curse God and die." Other experiences of pain and illness may generate questions of meaning and purpose in life as we attempt to survive. This is a microcosm of what some persons experience on an intermittent basis for the rest of their lives with chronic illness. Others do not have the same intensity, but are just as disabled or restricted in their functions. Questions of "Why?" and "What is the purpose of this illness?" often enter their minds. Some have been tremendously active only to find themselves able to do little after the illness. Life changes radically. The losses are horrific. Pain may be a constant companion. Dependency upon others may be necessary for survival. Self-esteem may plummet. There is emotional and spiritual crisis and trauma.

Social worker Irene Pullin, who had two children who died in their teens from congenital heart defects, has written of the impact she associates with chronic illness, as issues of control, self-image, dependency, stigma, abandonment, anger, isolation, and death.[6] It is estimated that approximately 15 percent of Americans have been diagnosed with a chronic illness. Since this percentage increases in the aged population and since our aged population is rapidly increasing, we can expect to see more people suffering from chronic illnesses in the decades ahead.

Chronic illnesses challenge many of our theological and spiritual ideas. They raise the issue of why there is human suffering, and can leave the patient feeling demoralized and hopeless. Anger at God for not intervening in providing a cure or healing can in turn bring feelings of guilt as the sick person and family members seek to deal with the reality before them.

Leahey and Wright give eight assumptions about families with chronic illness which can assist us in understanding. Some of these assumptions are as follows:

- There are predictable points of family stress. For example, when the disease conflicts with family developmental transitions such as when a disabled child has to begin school.
- Families vary in their levels of tolerance for the patient's condition.
- Families under stress tend to hold on to previously proved patterns of behavior, whether or not they are effective under current circumstances.
- Families usually go through a grief-loss process following the diagnosis of a disabling condition.
- Many families have difficulty adjusting to a chronic physical illness because of incorrect or inadequate disease-related information.
- In chronic illness, families must adjust to changed expectations of each other.
- A family's perception of the illness event is the greatest influence upon ability to cope.[7]

A time line for the phases of chronic illness has been developed.[8] The time phases are crises which include the prediagnostic period, the diagnosis, and the initial adjustment period. One of the tasks for the family during this period is to create a meaning for what has occurred and how it has changed the family identity. This includes loss and grief and certainly may raise some spiritual questions among the family members. The second phase, or chronic phase, involves the psychosocial, and I would add, the spiritual adaptation of the family. Of course, this period will vary in length according to the disease and its progression. It can be a time of uncertainty and struggle to maintain some type of normal family life in the midst of the upheavals of the disease. Finally, the terminal phase marks the period when death is inevitable. The family at this junction has to adjust to periods of grief, loss, and mourning.

When a family does not adapt well to one phase, chances are they will have problems during the later phases. At times, the family will get stuck in an adaptation that worked well in one phase, but no longer works at a later phase of the illness. For example, it is often adaptive to for the family to become more enmeshed during the crisis phase, but this may be too confining during the chronic phase.[9]

While this time line of the phases of chronic illness can vary tremendously from disease to disease and family to family, it is helpful in understanding some of the psychosocial and spiritual stressors such families endure. A careful understanding of the family and individual dynamics, as well as beliefs, is vital if we are to assist those going through such a crisis. We cannot apply our knowledge about one individual or family to all other families. However, general guidelines can assist us in being more observant of the stressors resulting from chronic illnesses.

THE IMPORTANCE OF PREVENTION

One positive change currently developing in the medical arena is a clearer emphasis on prevention. Preventive measures can help persons avoid some physical crises or at least delay them to later life. In the past, health care providers were not rewarded for teaching preventive health practices although many did so. The day is fast approaching (or already here in many areas) when it will benefit the provider to assist the patient in staying well by using preventive measures. Less utilization of medical care by patients will be a plus to providers. Therefore prevention is becoming cost-effective in the marketplace. Behavioral science has a lot to teach about assisting with prevention. In fact, I can see a strong partnership developing between behavioral medicine and preventive medicine. Consultation and collaboration between primary care physicians, mental health providers, pastoral counselors, and ministers could be effective ways of integrating these two important domains.

Currently, health care programs and financial constraints may be reducing the ability to deal with the total person and may be narrowing the focus to only the crisis point of a person's life. Hopefully, as health care companies develop a more comprehensive system, preventive medicine will force an emphasis on the whole person. Rather than just do crisis management of the patient, we will look at the broader influences on the patient's health. Eventually, the new leverage given to preventive measures will broaden our perspective of health and medicine. An emphasis on prevention should help us with better integration of the multicausal and multidimensional frameworks of life and health, including the spiritual. No longer can sickness be seen as an isolated event; it most often has some connection with the context and content of our lives.

Years ago Laframboise proposed that health is determined by four primary areas: environment, lifestyle, human biology, and the system of health care organization.[10] Other researchers have written that these four components have to be in balance for health to occur.[11] They all influence each other in a reciprocal process. Realizing this reciprocity, in this chapter, the lifestyle component will be our main focus.

The Importance of Lifestyle in Prevention of Crisis

Lifestyle includes such things as leisure activity risks, what we consume, and our health habits. Researchers say lifestyle behaviors influence at least 50 to 70 percent of premature deaths in this country. Emotional, spiritual, and psychological components that play an important role in one's lifestyle are often neglected by persons seeking to make changes, or health care providers encouraging change. There is mounting empirical evidence for the inclusion of the positive effect of religious and spiritual factors in health in addition to psychological and emotional factors which are now broadly recognized as important.[12] I believe that we do not put initiate or maintain many preventive measures for lack of addressing these psychological, emotional, and spiritual factors.

Matarazzo called high-risk behaviors that are harmful to health "behavioral pathogens," and health related behaviors that can reduce disease, enhance health, and perhaps contribute to the quality of life "behavioral immunogens."[13] Most of us do not have any difficulty identifying "behavioral pathogens" such as excessive alcohol use, high fat and cholesterol diets, and lack of exercise. Due to the health education by the media, most of us also know of lifestyle changes that would be to our health benefit. Our real difficulty is putting the "behavioral immunogens" or good health habits into practice. Most realize the importance of regular exercise. Why do the majority not exercise? Why do many who begin an exercise program quit after a day or two? Why do we fail to appreciate the importance of time for reflection and meditation? The benefits of wearing a seat belt are clear today. Why do some people not use them? On and on we could go with the lack of doing the "right thing" to improve our health status. The reasons for not improving are many, and sometimes complicated. We cannot adequately address all our obstacles to positive lifestyle reform in this chapter. However, let us look at a few psychosocial and belief system factors that may impact upon our ability and willingness to redirect our lives.

PSYCHOLOGICAL AND BELIEF SYSTEM ISSUES AFFECTING HEALTH BEHAVIOR

Self-Efficacy

Social learning theory has found that those who believe they can accomplish their goals can make changes easier. This is not based upon their actual ability, but upon their belief. Albert Bandura has called these efficacy expectations.[14] Efficacy expectations are expectations about the ability to perform the required behavior or "Can I do it?" Obviously, this question has a profound influence on a person's willingness to consider lifestyle modification and his or her endurance if attempting do so. Bandura also wrote of the importance of outcome expectations. Outcome expectations are basically the question, "What benefits will it bring me?" How the person thinks about the benefits and whether they are immediate or far into the future affects motivation for modifying behavior.

External versus Internal Locus of Control

Closely related to self-efficacy, locus of control refers to whether people feel they can make choices and influence change or whether they feel it is someone or something external that controls their lives, including the ability or inability to make transitions. The extreme of this is helplessness, the belief that nothing you can do will change what happens to you. Events have so traumatized some that, based on their life experiences, they feel they are helpless. This may have been true in the past and is generalized to all areas of life. Does the person have the belief that one's own behavior determines health or does he/she believe that factors beyond one's control determine health totally?

Personality Style

Some persons, for various reasons, live a life of immediate gratification and have very little discipline. They tend to be impulsive. This makes positive lifestyle transformation difficult and hard to maintain. Others have personality styles that continually keep them in conflict and chaos with little time to reflect and redirect their actions and behaviors into more productive goals. Helping them track these personality styles and offering them structure and accountability may be necessary before major lifestyle modifications can occur.

Cultural and Family Beliefs

Cultural or family beliefs or myths victimize some by inferring no change can occur for them. They may be the "black sheep" of their families and may have been told that they will never succeed. The dominant or more powerful group in society may enforce or reinforce the entrapment of certain persons into ghettos of despair and no opportunity. The impact of such factors on the psyche of persons can blind them to their true potential. Cultural and subcultural dynamics can be powerful obstacles to reformation.

Families may exert a powerful influence for a person not to change or to change back to an old patten. For example, persons who need to make dietary adjustments because of diabetes or heart disease may often fail with compliance. Frequently the family, not just the patient, needs to be educated about the needed dietary adjustments. Attempting to modify dietary habits while the family continues in the old patterns can be almost impossible. Context needs to be addressed.

Religious Beliefs and Social Norms

Religious belief, which has a tremendous potential for good, can on the other hand become a confining and limiting trap for some. Distorted religious beliefs that make one totally dependent upon others can limit positive behavioral change. Religious beliefs that expect God to do it all or that promote a complete split between the body and soul may have a very negative view about energy being put into self-care.

Social norms may promote certain destructive health and life-style behaviors that block more positive preventive behaviors from being explored. The person may have no one to model healthy behaviors or encourage positive habits. Media may promote such things as high-risk behavior, violence, or women's thinness to the detriment of many in our society.

Psychological and Emotional Dynamics

Certainly we recognize that this area has an impact on behavioral change. Depression, hopelessness, negative cognition, and anxiety can all be paralyzing in their effects. Cognitive therapy research has shown how negative and/or distorted thinking can maintain many prominent emotional disruptions and keep a person functioning below their potential.

Another powerful psychological dynamic is that of the risk of moving out of our "comfort zone." The familiar is easier even if destructive sometimes. Change is usually difficult even if it is good.

Self-Care and Self-Responsibility

Another area that needs to be addressed in promoting preventive measures is that of self-care and responsibility. Too often the past medical model has promoted a dependence on the medical establishment for health. Operating out of a disease model promoted this reliance on physicians and took away many people's sense of control over their health. We need a partnership where self-responsibility is encouraged and professionals are seen as support persons, not as those responsible for health. Helping people assume self-care in preventive practices is necessary as a way to assist them in realizing the control they do have over their health.

GROUPING BARRIERS TO PREVENTIVE HEALTH CHANGE

One way of grouping barriers to preventive health intervention or change, such as those just mentioned, is to put them into categories. Lawrence Green and others have used the categories of predisposing factors, enabling factors, and reinforcing factors.[15] Predisposing factors include a person's knowledge, attitudes, beliefs, values, and perceptions. These factors particularly have an influence on a person's *motivation*. Enabling factors include necessary skills, availability, and accessibility of health care providers and other health promoting resources. The enabling factors are important in *facilitation* of health care, prevention, and change. Reinforcing factors include family support, peer influence and support, health care provider support, and rewards for the change in behavior. These are important for *reinforcement* of positive behaviors. Obviously it is important that these all be addressed if one is to have the best opportunity for positive behavioral reform and preventive practices. If a person is very motivated to change and has access to a health care facility, but has no family support, he or she may have more difficulty making and maintaining any desired transformations.

From this very brief overview one can see there are individual-belief and social-environmental determinants of health and preventive practice. It is important that we consider both the individual and social if we are to help others with change or make change ourselves. Too often we have labeled persons who have difficultly making positive life adjustments as "resistant" or "noncompliant," or have even given them much worse labels without considering the powerful forces that may be at work to keep them operating in the same old patterns. Health care providers, counselors, and ministers may have unrealistic expectations for change in a patient, based on their lack of understanding the context of the patient's life. On the other hand, our expectations for change may be too low, based on experiences with other persons. Additionally, we may be too hard on ourselves when we fail to make our own desired changes. We may be too simplistic in our approach and not assess the commitment necessary and the multiple levels of reluctance in our personal worlds.

Phases of Health Change Behavior

Milsum has written about the phases in health behavioral change such as enthusiasm, discouragement, and stability.[16] One might think of the example of weight management. Many of us have had the excitement and enthusiasm of deciding to make a lifestyle change such as joining a weight-loss program. We imagine ourselves as we could look or would look with the weight loss, wearing new clothes, and so on. Invariably for many, however, the time eventually comes when the discouragement starts to set in: "Why should I be denying myself so much?—that ice cream sundae looks so good!" At that time the benefit of being able to get into new clothes does not seem so great and perseverance is greatly tested. A strong support system is needed at this time. We may want to warn the persons with whom we are working about this phase and have the patient come in for counseling when the discouragement hits. If the person can hang on and begin to feel and see the benefits of the weight loss, then it can become self-reinforcing. It may become easier to maintain the program of change. Some can probably maintain this state as a lifestyle. Others may relapse even at this point. Some may do well until life stressors become excessive and then relapse. Again, thinking about these phases and the potential for relapse emphasizes the importance of a multidimensional approach where factors from all areas of one's life are addressed to enhance the change potential. Bird, Christie-Seely, and Yaremko-Dolan have devised the diagram in Figure 9.2, which is a nice summary of many of the ways we have been approaching the subject matter of this chapter. They wrote the following in regard to this systemic diagram:

> Congruence between different areas and between systems results in tranquility. Major discrepancies result in guilt, anger, embarrassment, or conflict between systems (for example, individual and family conflict over religion or lifestyle, especially if individuation is low). Illness may result (an escape into a sick role or result of stress). Integration of all areas is complex and rarely fully achieved. Crisis or illness may represent disturbed homeostasis because of change in one area.[17]

FIGURE 9.2. Value Systems

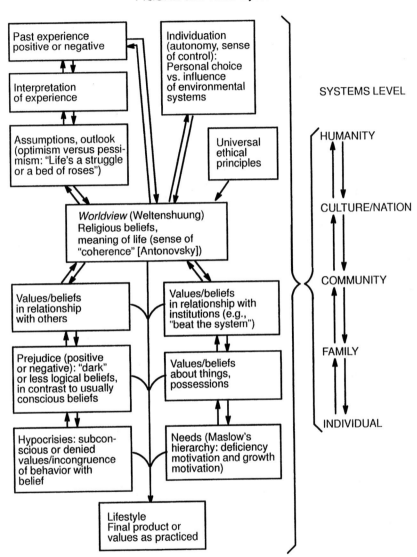

Looking at the larger picture when encouraging positive change in others or in ourselves is important. Simplistic fads and magical techniques rarely promote lasting change. A more holistic approach that incorporates the psychological, spiritual, and behavioral components both on an individual and social level is a much more powerful transforming agent. We need to adopt a model of change that promotes an overall positive lifestyle and an idea of wellness that is not just focused on absence of disease. Psychosocial aspects should be considered, discussed, and addressed. We can be an impetus in assuring that the psychosocial aspects of prevention are included—education and care. This will enhance the possibility of true lifestyle change which can lessen some of the crises of life.[18]

THE CHURCH AND PREVENTIVE HEALTH

The split between the spiritual and physical in western society has resulted in the church not addressing preventive health practices very well. Churches and denominations have been instrumental in founding hospitals and providing medical care for individuals here and abroad. Yet health education is only now beginning to become an activity of the church, except among a few denominations which have built a theology that includes this aspect of life. In less recent history the church was more involved in health beliefs, education, and practices: "Indeed, the delivery of what we now call human services was at one time the sole province of the churches and synagogues."[19] There are some churches that provide health screening and some are beginning to have a resident nurse on site. It appears to me that this is a valid ministry of the church. As stated above, lifestyle practices account for some estimated 70 percent of illnesses thus, much suffering could be prevented by a more healthful approach to living. In medicine and in the church, the focus has been on crisis intervention instead of seeking to educate in preventive health so that many physical crises could be avoided.

While we should not make health practices a test of fellowship or take a legalistic approach to health behavior, the church could and should have a greater impact in this arena. If there was something overtly killing and maiming our population by the hundreds of thousands the church would surely speak out to change this, but this is what is happening with unhealthful life-style practices. The research that has been done in this area in the last few decades encourages us to continue to explore this for it has revealed that: "there is a clear and undeniable influence that religion has on the prevention of illness and the promotion of health."[20]

This chapter emphasizes the impact of physical problems on the lives of individuals and families as well as spiritual influence. Therefore, the church should add to its ministry and education the importance of paying attention to the physical dimension of life. The changes coming in medicine and research are giving more and more emphasis to the connection between emotional states, meaning states or spiritual beliefs, and illness states. Larson refers to this as the discovery or rediscovery of the spiritual nature of people.[21] Some of the existential writers have stated for decades that purpose in life gives greater likelihood of survival under difficult circumstances.[22] The crisis of physical illness challenges the very purpose and meaning of life. The church, pastoral counselors, and ministers have a role to play in assisting individuals and families during illnesses and the resulting crises of meaning. "Do not be wise in your own eye; fear the Lord and shun evil. This will bring health to the body and nourishment to your bones."[23]

Questions for Discussion/Reflection

1. What questions come forth from persons going through a physical crisis?

2. What were some of the health beliefs in your family of origin? Who was the nonprofessional "health expert?" What were some of the home remedies?
3. What religious teaching were you exposed to regarding health and disease?
4. What are "explanatory models?"
5. Do you think the church should be involved in preventive health teachings?

Chapter 10

The Crisis of Religious Burnout

When one looks across the religious landscape it is shocking to see the vast number of traumas and casualties lying along the holy places. Persons who once centered their lives around their faith have forsaken it, or they have become as lifeless as mannequins in a store window. Some continue to repeatedly go through the movements that no longer have meaning to them.

This chapter will focus on the form versus the essence. There is a crisis that occurs when we confuse these that can disrupt and arrest our spiritual growth. It can happen slowly over time with a distraction of our awareness or it can occur more rapidly under powerful influences and control. Regardless, it can hemorrhage our spiritual lives.

Religion, of course, has great positive impact. History as well as anthropology and archeology have shown us how pervasive it is and has been throughout the world. It has been the means of facilitating the spiritual development of many peoples. Yet there is a shadow side of the use of religion. We are all aware of the great overt tragedies that have been done in the name of religion. However, there is another shadow side that is far more subtle. It can lead to a malady we might call "religious burnout."

This phenomenon is most easily seen in its extreme among the cults although it can occur in all religious movements. However,

---

The original version of this chapter appeared as "Mistaking Religion for Spirituality" in *The Pastoral Forum*, Volume 9, No. 1, 1990. Copyright by The Bradley Center, Inc. Used by permission.

in the cults one usually finds great pressure toward conformity and giving up of individuality. Originally new converts may artificially improve their functioning in some areas because they borrow ego strength from the belief system or group. They may become leaders for the "truth." Previously uncommitted persons, many become "true believers," to use Eric Hoffer's term, ready to sacrifice to any length for the group.[1] Often in this process there is a loss of selfhood, a giving up of personality, and a blunting of personal freedom.

When such persons are asked about how they are doing, they will give a positive answer. How could they be an example for "the truth" if they admit to feeling bad? A powerful denial structure comes into operation which may screen out whole segments of thoughts and feelings. They begin running on an obsession, a religious high, or what we might call a religious addiction.

ADDICTIVE PROCESSES IN ORGANIZATIONS

Although all religious systems might be called addictive to some extent, many can have addictive behaviors and can be used addictively by certain personalities. Some of the processes of addictive systems that are described by Ann Schaef are as follows:[2] First there is the process of the promise. By this she is referring to the focus on expectations and the future. This can give temporary relief from the present at the expense of keeping us out of touch with the present.

Second, there is the process of the pseudopodic ego which is the process of the organization absorbing all that is different from itself. Individuals within such organizations have difficulty saying "no."

Closely related to the above, external referencing is the third process Schaef gives. This refers to the tendency to define the self by focusing outside oneself to the group to which one belongs. Boundaries are lacking between the individual and the group. Individual feelings and desires are surrendered to those of the organization. They have difficulty setting limits for themselves and differentiating between themselves and the religious system.

The process of invalidation is another process used by the addictive organization in dealing with what the system cannot control or understand. Those opinions voiced which come into collision with the organization are ignored or dismissed. This is a means of control and another means of keeping individuals out of touch with their feeling and experience.

Dualism is another process used by addictive organizations and is often found among religious groups. This simplifies things down to two choices. Often this is an "us and them" or a "good and bad" mentality. This gives a sense of false security at the expense of not allowing more options. It also keeps one from exploring other alternatives.

Unfortunately, the processes described above are not only found among the cults and addictive systems, they are also in the religious institutions we attend. Effort of control, denial, conformity, invalidation, absorption, and so on can impinge upon the self, draining vitality and creativity. As one shuts down parts of selfhood, there can be a tendency to become locked within a narrow range of mechanical behaviors and feeling. The gradual loss of control to the larger system leaves one searching for places to find some feeling of control in life. More often than not, this is found by becoming more controlling and demanding to those nearest, such as family members. No longer is one acting out of love, but now is acting out of the aggression of knowing the "truth." Often lives of family members as well as one's own are stifled of life-enhancing spirituality.

Subtle emotional trauma occurs with this loss of selfhood. It may take years for the person involved to realize and admit the negative effects because of the strength of the denial system. However, often these persons slowly begin to burn out religiously.

Resources are taken from them without replenishment and survival becomes based on emotional numbness, leaving them empty and spiritually bankrupt. These persons become the bruised and wounded who eventually may see life and religion as tasks of futility.

THE PROBLEM OF MISTAKING RELIGION FOR SPIRITUALITY

The basis of the problem is this: Religion is used in the place of spiritual experience rather than being used as a tool to enhance spiritual development. Form is substituted for essence, conformity overrules individuality, the system crowds out God, and religion is mistaken for spirituality. Tony Campolo has written that when he became a Christian it was not "the world" that almost wrecked his faith, but the stifling expectations and demands of the religious in the church.[3]

A religion in which spirituality is hampered becomes controlling. It often has a "God in a box" mentality and does not allow members to think outside of the tight boundaries of the closed religious system. Individual initiative is barricaded behind the walls of the religious establishment.

On the other hand, spirituality motivates us toward growth and wholeness. It recognizes the freedom of each individual to make up his or her own mind. It affirms the right of all to think for themselves and live with their own personality and individuality. Spirituality allows for spontaneous and creative acts of worship. Rather than blunting the emotions and intellect, spirituality encourages the expression of our total humanity.

THE CHALLENGE

The challenge is for us to be willing to break through our own denial system and assess the contribution our religious organizations may make to the eventual religious burnout of their members. It may be frightening at times to step outside our traditional and prescribed ways of thinking, yet it may be necessary to avoid religious burnout. In contrast to the stifling and smothering of rigidified religion, the freedom of religion, which is a conduit for spirituality, can be exhilarating and energizing.

Questions for Discussion/Reflection

1. What are some roads that may lead to religious burnout?
2. Do you believe it is possible to develop a religious addiction?
3. What ways are our communities of worship similar or dissimilar to cults?
4. How would you differentiate religion and spirituality?
5. In what ways is your religious system too rigid? too unstructured?

Chapter 11

The Crisis of Psychological Disturbance

From earliest times there has been a fascination and a fear of mental illness. It has often been associated with a very negative prejudice. For example, early in history, it was associated with evil and evil spirits. The treatment among cave dwellers during the Stone Age was a method called trephining. This consisted of using crude instruments to chop a hole in the skull in order to allow the evil spirits to escape from the person.[1] Considering mental illness as an influence or possession of the gods or evil spirits was not out of context for early humankind since most things not understood were interpreted in this way.

The problem is that we still do not understand mental illness very well in some respects and continue to place negative associations upon those who are ill in this way. Sometimes they are still seen as evil or as precipitating their illnesses by not having enough faith or bad behavior. We still have many myths regarding mental illness as seen in Table 11.1. Such myths or beliefs create even more of a crisis for the family of the person with mental illness.

In this chapter we will briefly address the impact of chronic or severe mental illness on families and suggest that the church needs much more sensitivity in ministering to these families. Next we will give a cursory overview of some of the ways of assessing mental health from pastoral counseling models. Finally, we will look at some of the more common issues that can contribute to emotional and psychological difficulties which are also very prevalent in communities of worship.

TABLE 11.1. Some Popular Myths and Misconceptions Concerning Mental Disorder and Abnormal Behavior

Myth:	Fact:
Abnormal behavior is invariably bizarre.	The behavior of most individuals diagnosed with a mental disorder is usually indistinguishable from that of a "normal" person.
Normal and abnormal behavior are different in kind.	Few if any types of behavior displayed by mental patients are unique to them. Abnormality consists largely of a poor fit between behavior and the situation in which it is enacted.
As a group, former mental patients are unpredictable and dangerous.	A typical former mental patient is no more volatile or dangerous than a "normal" person. The exceptions to this rule generate much publicity and give a distorted picture.
Mental disorders are associated with fundamental personal deficiencies and hence they occur because individuals fail to correct a deficit.	So far as we know, everyone shares the potential for becoming disordered and behaving abnormally.
Appropriate attitudes toward mental disorders include awe and fearfulness about one's own foibles and vulnerability.	Mental disorders are natural adaptive processes that are comprehensible within this context. The majority of people have an excellent chance of never becoming disordered and of recovering completely should the unlikely happen.

Source: *Abnormal Behavior and Modern Life,* by Robert C. Carson and James Butcher, ninth edition, p. 6, Copyright 1992, by Harper-Collins Publishing, Inc. Reprinted by permission of Addison-Wesley Educational Publishers, Inc.

We need a much better informed and sensitive general approach to dealing with the psychologically ill. On the other hand, there are times when we have to be able to admit that "people who live in a recurrent or perpetual state of disorder irritate, aggravate, and frustrate us. They wear on our nerves. They enrage or depress us or alternately do both."[2] One reason this may be so is because we see parts of ourselves in them and have a fear of becoming more like them.

THE IMPACT OF MENTAL ILLNESS ON THE FAMILY

While the problems mentioned previously can certainly be serious and painful, sometimes they are temporary, and they can often be addressed and interventions can be attempted. Some more serious forms of mental disturbance may not change or may have the unpredictability of episodic chaos. It is estimated that one in four families is affected by some mental illness. The crisis of severe mental or emotional illness upon a family is often devastating: "The problems with my daughter were like a black hole inside of me into which everything else had been drawn. My grief and pain were so intense sometimes that I barely got through the day."[3] John McCannon, who was formerly president of the Georgia chapter of National Alliance for the Mentally Ill and has a son who is a paranoid schizophrenic, wrote of his family's experience. I have gleaned a few of the main points he makes:

- The family believes their situation is unique.
- The family's experience is indescribably painful.
- Myths regarding mental illness cause many misunderstandings.
- The family experiences prolonged grief, frustration, helplessness, and anxiety.
- Parents often feel a sense of guilt and failure.
- There is bewilderment, embarrassment, and secrecy.
- Families become isolated with little social life.
- Reactions of churches or synagogues make it difficult to believe God cares.
- Often underlying emotions fester and spiritual distrust develops.
- Feelings are sometimes confusing and frightening.[4]

From this it is easy to begin to recognize the difficultly of living with a family member who has a severe mental illness. It can be a serious trauma which impacts all family members. Other people do not understand, our society does not promote understanding, and even our religious institutions have not ministered well in this area. Stewart Govig sent a survey to families with mentally ill members and received some examples of positive support from churches, but also received replies such as: "The pain is so terrible . . .", "One would be happy to have your minister even be willing to admit that there are mentally ill in the congregation . . ." and "Most people I have talked to have received either *no* help or *negative* avoidance from their clergy."[5] The families who responded reported desiring clergy and congregation involvement. We need to find ways to be present to such families without giving false assurance that things will get better. They need to know we care and that we will not condemn them for their honest questionings and doubts.

ASSESSMENT FROM A PERSPECTIVE THAT INCLUDES THE SPIRITUAL

Raup has suggested that theology and psychology have several concepts related to pathology in common but they are described with different language.[6] Both assess the relationship between the person and a significant other, the distortion with reality, splitting (theologians focus on interpersonal, psychologists on intrapersonal), self-centeredness or narcissism, extremes (deviance, antinomianism), values, and dependence. The church and psychology have often been at odds, yet there is much that is parallel in these disciplines. A bridging of theology and mental health could result in a much more comprehensive understanding of the person and greater ministry to the human condition. We have created too great a gulf between the behavioral sciences and the church.

There have been various ways of attempting to assess mental health. Most of these have focused on pathology and have given rise to a labeling process that is often not helpful and may even be destructive. The "Bible" of the mental health profession, *The Diagnostic and Statistical Manual of Mental Disorders,* has largely ignored the relationship, family, and spiritual context of a person's life. Pastoral counseling and other branches of psychotherapy have sometimes given a more holistic approach which includes the spiritual. Although no attempt is made here to be comprehensive, a few of the more holistic approaches to assessment are mentioned below.

Pruyser's Diagnostic Categories

Pruyser gave the following diagnostic categories. Even though these are put in more theological language Pruyser states that God-talk or theological language is not needed in order to hear these areas of a person's life.[7]

1. *Awareness of the Holy:* This involves what the person reveres. It is associated with having a sense of awe and the mystical. This area can involve beliefs about God and meaning in life.
2. *Awareness of Providence:* How does the person view the world and life? Is it seen as good or bad, friendly or unfriendly? While recognizing the bad in the world can the person also see some purpose and plan? Can the person trust? Can the person trust not only God, but others including pastors and counselors?
3. *Experience of Faith:* Does the person deal with the realities of life by taking legitimate risks or does he or she go to the extreme of being overly cautious and critical? Is there a sense of some type of commitment?
4. *Sense of Grace/Gratefulness:* Does the person have a sense of gratitude and appreciation? Does he or she understand

giving and receiving? Does the person forgive self and others? Is grace a response or a duty?

5. *Experience of Repentance:* This area deals with the process of change. Does the person have a sense of a need to change? Does the person at times feel a need to grow? Is there a sense of one's own contribution to problems?

6. *Sense of Communion:* This involves caring and feeling cared for by others. Is there a sense of connectedness with others?

7. *Sense of Vocation:* This is related to Erikson's concept of generativity. Does the person want to make a contribution to society, to be involved in the world? What is the sense of the person's involvement in constructive activities?

Oates' Thematic Approach to Assessment

Wayne Oates gave a thematic approach to assessment which included the following:

1. In the beginning—This includes what feelings people have about being born, blessings and curses, and what they feel they were meant to be.

2. The way things have been—This includes who they turn to for help, what is most difficult to forget, and recent stressors.

3. The way things are now—This includes what they think has been the greatest injustice to them, what hinders them, the biggest mystery to them, the greatest temptation, the thing they are most afraid of, and who they blame for their troubles.

4. The way things can change—This includes if people believe things can change, if they believe in luck, magic, or chance, how they feel, and what they would change if they were magicians?

5. What is their conception of God?

6. How they feel about the church—This includes settled beliefs that they believe will not change for them.[8]

Carroll Wise has stated that for pastoral evaluation there are actually three aspects of reality to assess. First is the person's concept of the ultimate reality and how this functions in his or her life. Second is the person's concept of reality of the external world. Last is the person's own inner world.[9]

Examining the way a person uses religion can be a barometer of mental health.[10] Often we see a basically healthy belief system that has been distorted or modified to serve the ends of psychological problems.[11] Too often religion gets a bad rap by the presentation of the more bizarre beliefs of the mentally ill. Psychotics have more bizarre and spectacular characteristics that often involve a religious component.[12] While we all distort reality and have contradictions of beliefs and behaviors, these can be more extreme among the mentally ill. It is important to remember that persons who have pathological illnesses can use religion pathologically.

CONSIDERATIONS FOR MINISTERING TO THOSE IN THE CHURCH

Clebsch and Jaekle give four areas of pastoral care in the church: healing, or restoring the person to wholeness, sustaining, or helping persons endure when cure is unlikely, guiding, or assisting persons with spiritual direction during times of perplexity, and fourth, reconciling, or assisting in the restoring of relationships.[13] These are vital areas for addressing the needs of those in the church. However, it is important that we not assume that all within the church have the same stories or the same ways of understanding. While there are commonalities in stressors and emotional strains we all experience, it would be a mistake to see church members as machines on an assembly line all in need of the same adjustment. This is one of the problems with approaches that tell everyone to just have enough faith or "get right with God and everything will be all right."

As mentioned in Chapter 9, Arthur Kleinman uses the term "explanatory model" to describe the worldview of persons or their interpretive framework for viewing the world. We all have various explanatory models based upon our experiences, our models of meaning, and our belief systems. Berger and Luckmann discussed how societies have "subuniverses of meaning" which define our experience of reality.[14] All churches and denominations have their own subcultures or subuniverses of meaning, so it is important to understand their behavior within its context. "Churches have their own language, nonverbal symbols, codes, norms, and patterns of relationships—their own cultures. If professionals have not been a part of this cultural context, they will find themselves, for all practical purposes, in a cross-cultural practice setting."[15] Seeking to understand a person's religious or spiritual context is as important as any other part of individual history such as ethnicity, race, socioeconomic status, and so on.

Without in any way meaning to be disrespectful to those who suffer from severe distortions of reality, and since we all suffer this to one degree or another, I would like to illustrate this point by a story:

> There once was a man who thought he was a kernel of corn. So each time he saw a rooster he would panic and run like crazy for fear the rooster would eat him. His relatives finally sought a noted psychiatrist to treat him at a mental hospital. The psychiatrist worked daily with the man to help convince him that he was not a kernel of corn.
>
> Finally the day came when the psychiatrist asked the man, "Are you a kernel of corn?" To this the man replied, "No I am not a kernel of corn. I know I am not a kernel of corn." There was great rejoicing in the hospital because the man was cured of his faulty belief. So, they discharged the man from the hospital and he was on his way home when he saw a rooster. He immediately took off running as fast as he

could in the opposite direction. His family finally caught up with him and promptly and angrily took him back to the psychiatrist. The psychiatrist said to the man, "I thought I had convinced you that you are not a kernel of corn." "Yes," said the man, "I know that and you know that, but does the rooster know that?"

Those treating this man had missed an important part of his worldview. They thought that if they could change his thinking about himself all would be well. They didn't consider how he might perceive others (in this case a rooster) were thinking about him! This is the reason the broader assessment questions given above need to be used and why we need to hear each person's story in context.

Some Unhealthy Ways of Thinking and Being Often Found in the Church

With the caveat above, it does appear to me that some meaning states bring more problems of living than others. Most psychological illnesses will not be specifically addressed in this chapter except for the above cursory generalization of their impact on families. However, some of the unhealthy ways of psychological thinking and being that can lead us down the road to an eventual spiritual and emotional crisis are the following:

The Crisis of Pollyanna Delusions—Denial

First there is the crisis of Pollyanna Delusions. Some persons and families have a powerful dynamic at work in which they always have to say everything is going well. Anything bad or negative is denied. Although it is important to think of the positive as the apostle Paul says "whatever is true. . . . Think on these things,"[16] we must also be realistic and not blinded to situations that need to be addressed.

Although we have differing temperaments and optimism/pessimism tendencies, we should seek to balance out our personalities. An unrealistic optimism that too often uses denial may set us up for disappointment. There is the story of the twin brothers, exactly alike except that one was eternally optimistic, the other always pessimistic. The parents decided to test the extent of the pessimism and optimism of their twins. They bought a large box of toys and put it in the room of the twin who was always pessimistic, and bought a large box of manure and put it in the room of the optimist. They took the boys to their rooms and left them there to find the respective boxes. After a period of time the parents went to the room of the twin who was a pessimist to see how the box of toys had affected him. They opened the door and were surprised to find the little fellow sitting in the middle of the floor crying and sobbing heavily. When the parents inquired what was the matter, their son replied that these were all new toys and someday they would break and have to be thrown out. They comforted their son the best they could, then went to check on the son who had the box of manure placed in his room. To the surprise of the parents, when they opened the door, manure was being thrown all over the place as the little boy was digging furiously in the box. He was thrilled and with excitement said to his parents, "With all this manure there has to be a pony in here someplace!" Obviously, this little fellow was setting himself up for a disappointment.

We all use denial as a defense mechanism and denial can be a very important part of good mental health. However, some do push it to an extreme. The denial becomes a way of avoiding the difficulties and realities of life. It is a set-up for a major fall or spiritual earthquake. One way we do this is by believing that if we live right, pray enough, or have enough faith, nothing bad will happen to us. There is a healthy assurance about life that comes from faith and trusting in God. However, when this becomes a way of ignoring the perplexities, contradictions, and ambiguities of life, it may no longer be a sign of health.

When this extreme denial is finally penetrated by a crisis or the longtime wear and tear of life, a spiritual crisis can occur. It may be a prime time to fall prey to self-blame for not having prayed enough, not living close enough to God, or for not having enough faith. This on top of the current crisis, can send the person into a deep, dark hole of despair. It is much better to realize and confront the fact that life is not fair, just, or always good for the person of belief or anyone else. The Pollyanna attitude can be an escape from difficulties and therefore an escape from growth.

The Crisis of Projection—The Devil Made Me Do It

James Framo, a pioneer in the field of marriage and family therapy, wrote that in couple relationships we often project the unwanted parts of ourselves onto our mates and then fight them in our mates.[17] We all have parts of ourselves that are difficult for us to acknowledge, admit, or bring into our awareness. Jung called this the shadow side.

Christ confronted this with the words, "You hypocrite, first take the plank out of your own eye, and then you will see clearly to remove the speck from your brother's eye."[18] This crisis of projection is rampant in some churches with criticism running wild in the aisles. Sometimes it falls under the critical or mean spirit approach; other times it goes under the banners of "the devil made me do it" or "the devil is making them do it."

Often the reason some are most intensely critical of the behavior of others is because they are unconsciously desiring to participate in the behavior themselves. Projection is a defense that gives our unwanted and unacceptable motives or desires to another. It can keep the focus off our own internal conflict and for a time at least keep us feeling better about ourselves.

The projection of blame onto others for our behaviors is not only a characteristic of children, we adults can play this game also. Adam blamed Eve; Eve blamed the serpent. We do not like to admit to our own failure, betrayals, and sins. This also tends to get into an us/them approach which has often been a destructive force in churches. Healing cannot come while we ignore our own need for healing and/or correction.

The Crisis of External Locus of Control— Expecting God to Do It All

Another personal spiritual crisis is on the horizon when people expect God or someone else to do it all. These beliefs cause us to feel we have to be at the fate of forces beyond our control. While there is truth in this, it is certainly not the whole truth. In most circumstances there is something we can change, influence, or master. Victor Frankl found some semblance of control even in the concentration camps.[19]

Often persons who have an external locus of control become pessimists. They tend to believe the worst, to look for the bad to happen. Martin Seligman points out that the basis of pessimism is helplessness, which occurs when people believe that nothing they do will affect what happens to them. He states:

> . . . twenty-five years of study has convinced me that if we *habitually* believe, as does the pessimist, that misfortune is our fault, is enduring, and will undermine everything we do, more of it will befall us than if we believe otherwise. I am also convinced that if we are in the grip of this view, we will get depressed more easily, we will accomplish less than our potential, and we will even get physically sick more often. Pessimistic prophecies are self-fulfilling.[20]

I have had clients who have confirmed this to me over and over. Joe was very suicidal when I started working with him.

Suicide was functional for him in that when in a bind he planned to commit suicide and then he was able to have a carefree attitude about life. He continually felt that nothing he could do would change the course of his life. Then he set about bringing this self-fulfilling prophecy about by not planning for life, but by reacting to it. The only control he could feel initially was in planning his own suicide.

When we feel that life is totally uninfluenced by us, we feel like pawns moved about by the wrathful hand of fate or circumstance. Many who feel this way were excessively controlled as children and as a result they believe they can choose nothing for themselves as adults.

Another take on this is believing that everything is up to God. God is expected to do everything for us. "If I don't get a job, God didn't want me to have it even though I didn't go on the interview!" "When God wants my life to end, He will end it; it doesn't matter if I attempt to take care of my health or not." This can set up an apathetic approach to life as well as an eventual crisis of anger and blaming of God for what does not work well in our lives.

My parents have a worldview that is a result of their religious faith which I viewed as simplistic for a long time. It parallels to some extent Romans 8:28: "And we know that in all things God works for the good of those who love him . . ." They believe that things will work themselves out eventually. This usually works in reality! Most things do work out. But we cannot just always sit back and expect someone else to rescue us. We must participate in the plan and the action.

The Crisis of Legalism—Control

The great destroyer of happiness in many people of faith has been legalism. Legalism is a religion of human achievement. I like the way part of the first chapter of Galatians is interpreted by Wesley Nelson:

True liberation is an act of God. It is the exact opposite of all our struggles to achieve freedom by a show of superior strength . . . he [Christ] is not on the side of the enslavement that prevails among both the moral and immoral people when they seek to earn their acceptance by conforming to approved patterns of conduct.[21]

Legalism initially gives a pseudo feeling of being in control with accomplishments. It gives the feeling of being correct or righteous. But this does not last long for there is always a greater demand that comes over the horizon and beckons conformity. We strive to do, to be accepted by others, or by God. Our world revolves around performance of duty. We are attempting to feel secure by being in control and doing all the right things.

Often this leads us to criticize others to make us appear better so we can feel good about ourselves. But the good emotions from feeling "holier" than others do not last. The other dead-end route of legalism is ultimate despair. Once we realize that we cannot perform well enough or perfectly and that we will make mistakes in life, our basis for acceptance is shattered.

The Crisis of Instability and Insecurity—Anxiety

Many events in life can disrupt our view of how the world should operate. These events may throw us into a crisis of instability and insecurity. Anxiety is the emotional disorder of our time. It is one of the most frequent responses of our lives, and can cause us to be fearful and apprehensive. I have had clients tell me, "I live with an overriding feeling of fear in my life." Anxiety may even involve obsessions and compulsions. Religious rituals may be used as an expression of these obsessions and compulsions. This can be incapacitating and handicapping.

Although persons with severe anxiety disorders may require medication, the more positive statements of Christ such as "Therefore, do not worry about tomorrow, for tomorrow will worry about itself"[22] and ". . . surely I am with you always. . . ."[23] are actually not too far from the most common therapy used to deal with anxiety—cognitive therapy. Cognitive approaches assist in interrupting negative automatic thoughts. The cognitive approach also looks at core beliefs or schemes. A core belief is a belief we have about ourselves or the world that is a part of us. It may be one such as: "Something bad is going to happen." These beliefs influence our reactions and our interpretations of events.

Paul Tillich wrote of three types of anxiety: the anxiety of nonbeing or regarding fate and death, the anxiety of emptiness and meaninglessness, and the anxiety of guilt and condemnation.[24] He saw the anxiety over fate and death as the most basic since it is inescapable. He found a dominant form of anxiety at various periods in history among changes of societal structures of meaning and belief. For example, he saw moral anxiety or anxiety over guilt and condemnation as the main form of anxiety at the end of the Middle Ages with the breakdown of absolutism. In our age the anxiety of emptiness and meaninglessness dominates: "the anxiety of annihilating openness of infinite, formless space into which one falls without a place to fall upon."[25]

Anxiety robs us of our peace. Our very fast-paced overstimulating existence with its lack of emphasis on meditation, prayer, and communion contributes to our tension. Anxiety may be a message for us to slow down and focus on what really matters or address issues we have been neglecting in our personal and spiritual lives. Avoiding the messages anxiety is trying to give us may lead to serious crises in our lives.

The Crisis of the Inflated Self—Narcissism

Narcissistic personality disorder is the extreme of the inflated self and is resistant to change. But some have an inflated self that is more easily addressed. Once I had a couple in therapy and the guy said, "She loves me and so do I." He was not speaking of a healthy appreciation and love of self, but of being in love with himself. We all need a love of ourselves and Christ said, "Love your neighbor as you love yourself," indicating that self-love can be healthy. However, what we are talking about here can be destructive to self and to relationships.

We find in the biblical story of Adam and Eve, a reference to their desire to be as God, which was the first step to their downfall. They wanted to ". . .be as God, totally self-contained, self-sufficient, and needing no one and nothing from anyone. . . . The cryptic thread of narcissism runs through all our natures."[26] A narcissistic person in one of my churches made up his own loose standards of behavior for himself while believing that much more rigid standards should be imposed on others. He was above the rules. He had an extra special connection to God according to his self-report. While most, I hope, do not go to this extreme, many of us do have some of this inflated sense of ourselves. This can set us up for a huge downfall as has especially happened to many religious leaders who made special exceptions for their wrong behaviors. We all need the accountability of a caring and loving community that has the fortitude to challenge us when we push the limits too far.

The inflated self usually covers a very insecure self, a self that feels very inadequate and unaccepted. The inflation is a way to temporarily avoid dealing with these very painful feelings. It is much better to deal with the realities of our feelings and thoughts with trusted friends who can assist us in walking through them.

The Crisis of Condemnation—Guilt

Some of the most troubled of persons are disturbed by guilt. Many are living with self-condemnation from past acts. Others suffer from an oversensitive conscience which emotionally beats them over every imagined imperfection. Churches have used guilt as a means of motivation and control for centuries. This has wreaked havoc and destruction in many lives. Narramore has written candidly and clearly that he believes some false guilt feelings are destructive and that they can be a barrier to spiritual growth.[27] Guilt feelings can stifle human relationships, feelings of self-worth, and emotional health and growth as well.

Valid guilt feelings occur when we have truly done wrong. However, the confusion enters when many judge themselves wrong when they actually have no objective guilt. Others have continually disregarded their values to the point that the signal of guilt is no longer felt. They are like the person who has no pain sensors, no signal to stop or change behavior.

Narramore has constructed the diagram in Figure 11.1 to illustrate the similarities between guilt before God and the guilt we acquire as a result of failure to meet the standards of others (or ourselves). Either process can result in guilt feelings. Narramore states that if we substitute the failure to live as parents or others expect us in the initial steps in the diagram (regarding sin and objective guilt before God), it will modify the diagram to show how guilt feelings may grow out of relationships. He emphasizes how important it is to distinguish between objective guilt (true guilt for wrongdoing) and guilt feelings (which may be imposed by ourselves or others and are not the result of actual wrongs).[28] It is important to realize that there can be valid or invalid guilt before God and others. The conscience is not always perfect and has to be heard along with counsel and dialogue in community with others.

The Crisis of Conformity—Mindlessness

Ellen Langer describes mindlessness as a psychological roadblock that causes us to become like automatons trapped in old mindsets. She goes on to say this "is rooted in mindsets—unquestioning attitudes formed when we first hear certain information. . . . Because they lock us into one interpretation of a bit of information, mindsets prevent choice."[29] Mindlessness and its often resulting conformity run rampant in some church circles. Members do not really think much for themselves and certainly do not venture far outside the boundaries of what is often narrow

FIGURE 11.1. Guilt and Godly Sorrow

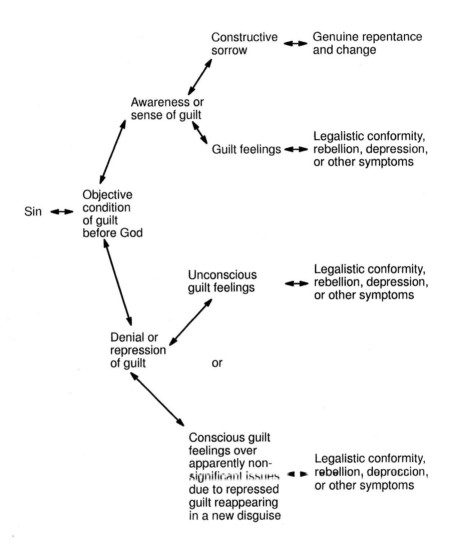

Source: *No Condemnation* by S. Bruce Narramore, p. 164. Copyright 1984 by the Zondervan Corporation. Used by permission of Zondervan Publishing House.

theological walls. "A closed system results in closed minds. The faithful are not supposed to—and in most cases dare not—think outside the boundaries of the closed theological system."[30]

Certainly we can find parallels in the scriptures to mindlessness. Many of the religious of Jesus' day could not venture outside of their prescribed thinking patterns. Even when Jesus used the teaching method of parables to attempt to get around some of their restricted hearing, often it did not work.

In her book Langer gives some of the potential problems of mindlessness:

- a narrow self-image
- self-induced dependence
- compartmentalization of uncomfortable thoughts
- loss of control
- learned helplessness
- stunted potential[31]

Langer calls the opposite of mindlessness "mindfulness," which involves the ability to look at issues with openness and to see varying points of view. None of us are completely mindful and this is certainly true in the church. This can be a set up for many personal crises, including leaving us more susceptible to those who would abuse their power.

THE USE OF SPIRITUALITY AND RELIGION IN PSYCHOLOGICALLY HEALTHY WAYS

As mentioned at the beginning of this chapter, psychologically unhealthy people often use spirituality and religion in unhealthy ways (also see Chapter 10). However, spirituality and religion, when appropriate, can be healthy psychological components of life. Wayne Oates gives several characteristics of this: (1) Comprehensiveness or the ability to maintain relationships with persons of differing opinions and beliefs. I think this also includes being open to the various aspects of living and not limiting our perspectives to one area of life. (2) Seeking or maintaining a curiosity about what one does not know. This also includes a willingness to learn and grow. (3) Ambiguity tolerance or the ability to tolerate the "many-colored spectrums of truth." (4) A sense of humor is another characteristic Oates gives of a healthy religious faith. This includes the celebration that is found among healthy religions. (5) Last, graduation is the term he uses for the healthy opportunity to grow from one level of faith to another without being rejected or disowned. Additionally, Oates gives the following as constants found in healthy religion: some under-standing of suffering that promotes community, hope, basic trust, and curiosity.[32]

Xavier lists the characteristics of mature spirituality as authen-ticity, compassion, responsibility, discipline, self-respect, realis-tic sense of guilt, and cooperative/creative approaches in rela-tionships. He describes the dynamic factors of mature spirituality as courage, love, and wisdom which he sees as interconnected.[33]

Psychological disturbance can be closely linked with a distor-tion of spirituality and religion. However, I would want to bal-ance this statement with my belief that psychological health is often closely linked with a proper relationship with spirituality and/or religion.

This chapter has addressed in a limited fashion one of the most avoided areas of ministry in the church—that of emotional health and illness. We need to bring this area of life into the church without all the superstitions and prejudices of the past. In the day of disappearing mental health insurance benefits for many, the church has a responsibility as well as an opportunity to have a profound ministry to those who are in emotional crisis.

Questions for Discussion/Reflection

1. Why do you think we continue to have such prejudices about psychological disturbance?

2. How open are most communities of faith to the pain of psychological problems? Do you think they are usually seen as failures of belief or faith?

3. What are some of the common distorted ways of thinking found in communities of faith that lead to emotional crisis?

4. How does legalism impact on psychological health? absolute freedom?

5. Are religion and spirituality psychological crutches?

Chapter 12

The Crisis of Personal Identity

THE SEARCH FOR DIRECTION AND MEANING

I once saw an old dilapidated bus that had been converted into a camper. Where the destination sign had always been shown in more glorious days of the bus was the word "Nowhere." Sometimes that is the story of our lives. We question if we are really going anywhere. Many today are wandering aimlessly down the dark pathway that once seemed to be so bright and clear. The society of which they are a part has become complicated and impersonal so they are without direction.

Our culture has a profound impact upon the personal identities of most in our society. The rapidity with which change is progressing leaves few tried and true procedures that are still surviving. Many career positions are outdated almost as fast as persons can complete training for them. Relationships and marriages break up and the history and continuity is lost. We are increasingly mobile and relocate frequently. Even meanings are changing. Some are echoing the words of Solomon: "Meaningless! Meaningless! . . . Utterly meaningless! Everything is meaningless."[1]

I remember when I was in an undergraduate sociology class and first heard the word "anomie" described to me. It involves a lack of purpose or identity. In sociology it often refers to society, but it can also refer to individuals. What is happening to our personal identities? Who are we? What is this all about? For many there is a crisis of personal identity. Some can readily acknowledge and describe it. Others simply have a vague questioning of "Is this all there is for my life?"

Clinebell, drawing from the work of Glasser, discussed human needs as the need to experience an authentic dependable personal relationship, the need for a sense of worth, the need to live responsibly, the need for inner freedom, the need for a sense of meaning, and the need for a loving, trusting relationship with God.[2] Fulfillment of these needs helps formulate our identities and yet they are so often left unfulfilled in our culture.

This chapter will examine personal identity crisis. As my sociology professor explained years ago, it is a problem of modern society. However, the church and pastors and pastoral counselors should have something to say regarding this crisis. I will suggest that, for Christians, redemptive history is the crux out of which our identity emerges.

THE IMPORTANCE OF BALANCE IN RELATIONSHIPS FOR IDENTITY FORMATION

Erikson uses identity in preference to self or ego as a way of expanding the concept of self to include the wider arena of social factors.[3] One thesis of this chapter is that identity is built on relationship and social influences.

Berger refers to the dialectical nature of development which fits well with the statements we have made about transitions and about extremes in other chapters. Berger uses an anxiety-security/competence-growth polarity for the discussion of the opposing areas of identity development. "Departure from a known or secure self at any particular point in time has the potential to arouse anxiety."[4] The anxiety polarity pulls toward the security of something in which to believe. Berger refers to Erikson's term used for some adolescents who are frantic for security, "identity diffusion," as an example of this. On the other hand, the competence polarity pushes toward growth, change, and integration.

Gerkin notes a similar polarity which he states is the tension between continuity and change that is a part of identity.[5]

In forging an identity, identifications with others are internalized. Identification in the social world is internalized by modeling after others.[6] Berger states that the identifications emotionally laden with competence promote integration of identity and those with anxiety block integration and wholeness. Identifications laden with anxiety may be becoming more prevalent in our modern society. We may be lacking in proper identifications for our children and for ourselves, thus fragmenting our very lives.

As stated in another context, this results in pieces of our selfhood being lost in various ways such as:

- Some of them were taken away by our parents or caretakers, in an attempt to turn us into what they thought we should be.
- Some of them we have given away to others in an attempt to be accepted or loved.
- Some of them we have hidden away, frightened of what others might think if they knew our secret lives.
- And some of them we have simply forgotten about, because we have been trying so hard to be something other than who we really are.[7]

ATTACHMENT REACTIONS THAT FORM PSEUDOIDENTITIES

Because of the issues raised above some have fused themselves with persons of power, status, and popularity; others simply submit their true selves to the whims and directives of others. Some have fused with organizations, even with the church. This gives a pseudoidentity at the expense of the growth that can come out of learning their own identity. What we are seeing in our society are persons who have identified so strongly with others that they have never defined themselves and, on the other hand, a lack of healthy relationships that provide a sense of our true selves.[8]

Codependency

Codependency is a popular term today. The word arrived on the scene and spread throughout our therapeutic vocabulary like a prairie fire. It has been used to describe everything from enabling an alcoholic to whatever. Even with its hodgepodge of meaning, as evidenced by its popular usage, it must be touching on some aspect of our lives that we feel. Codependency can be defined as ". . . an unhealthy pattern of relating based on low self-esteem and on the belief that one's worth depends on attachment to or the approval of some other person or group.[9]

The following have been compiled by Hogg and Frank as some of the behaviors associated with codependence:

- Martyrdom—sacrifice of one's own needs to meet the perceived needs of others.
- Fusion—loss of one's own identity in intimate relationships.
- Intrusion—control of other's behaviors through caretaking, guilt, and manipulation.
- Perfection—unrealistically high expectations of oneself and others.
- Addiction—use of compulsive behaviors for emotional self-control.[10]

These are certainly manifestations of an identity crisis. There is a loss of self and a lack of differentiation from others and even from institutions and structures. Too often there is fusion with others, institutions, careers, and so on.[11]

Codependency and the Church

Some have become codependent with the church. Life is centered around the church in such a way that this takes the place of self-identity or even worship of God. One author traced such a process through the Judeo-Christian history and shows that this is not just a modern problem.[12] He gave the example of the worship of the temple instead of the God of the temple that existed during Jeremiah's time and the worship of the scriptures without seeing the Messiah during the time of Christ. It is possible for persons to become obsessed with the church and feel dependent upon it for our survival.

There are churches that appear to encourage this dependency in an unhealthy way. Much damage has been done to individuals and their families in these situations, in the name of dedication to the church. Although for most there is not much danger of this happening since most today go to the other extreme and are distant from the activities of the church, it is a dynamic that needs attention. There is a difference between healthy and unhealthy involvement in the church. Church or cults that swallow up a person's individuality as well as their lives can destroy the gifts of the various members and produce robot-like xerox copies of each other. There may be unity at the expense of true self-identities. While we may have the same redemptive history we do not and cannot have the same individual narratives:

> Narrative identity is unsubstitutable; it cannot be given to someone else. There are no two people of whom the same narrative can be told; no two people who do and undergo the same acts and circumstances. Names, titles, and offices are identities which apply to more than one person, but there is no narrative of sufficient depth, "fraught with background," that picks out more than one person.[13]

Contradependence

The other side of the story is that of contradependence. Hogg and Frank have given a useful model to understand codependence and its counterpart contradependence. Too often we have focused on codependence or needs for affiliation and have not looked so carefully at the other side of the coin, the need for differentiation or contradependence. As depicted in Figure 12.1, the healthy integration of these is interdependence. Contradependence is defined by Hogg and Frank as attempting to separate from others to avoid being emotionally hurt. They list behaviors of contradependence as being some of the following:

- Defensiveness—use of psychological defenses to deny ownership of emotions or behaviors.
- Self-sufficiency—denial of emotional needs in relationships with others.
- Isolation—withdrawal from intimate relationships.
- Acting out—use of blaming, rage, or defiant behaviors to hurt or control others.

It can be seen immediately that codependents often have a lack of well-defined boundaries while contradependents often have more closed boundaries. "Codependence and contradependence become the adaptive exaggerations of the otherwise healthy motivations for love and autonomy."[14] The model given in Figure 12.1 can provide a useful diagram of balance. I have worked with persons who have been at one extreme and who attempt to move toward a more healthy approach only to go to the other extreme. Hogg and Frank describe this as a model to guide in learning the art of giving and receiving in relationships and providing changes in ego boundaries. The lower half of the diagram represents those who are very needy and find unhealthy ways to meet these deficits such as extreme codependence, contradependence, and use of addictive substances. The top half of the diagram reveals the balance of interdependence which is a positive interpersonal model. Such individuals can be close to others yet maintain their individuality. They can also be dependent or independent in healthy ways, but do not remain stuck in these modes of relationship interaction.

FIGURE 12.1. Model of Codependence and Contradependence

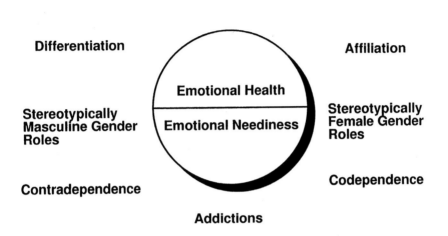

Source: Toward a Model of Codependence and Contradependence by James Hogg and Mary Lou Frank, *Journal of Counseling and Development,* 70, 1992, p. 373. Copyright American Counseling Association (ACA). No further reproduction authorized without written permission of ACA.

Boundaries

This is all very relevant to the concept of identity. We establish our identity in large part by defining our boundaries. By having proper boundaries we can define who we are, what we want, and what we need. Boundaries define our limits and thus what we do and do not desire or need. Without boundaries we end up identifying too strongly with others and living out of their desires and needs. Some who had a role reversal in childhood in which they were the main nurturer rather than the parent, easily fall into the role of knowing the needs of others, but have a lack of understanding of their own needs.

On the other hand, too many boundaries cut us off from the feedback and nurturance of others which can also limit our understanding and feedback about ourselves. Either of these extremes can bring a crisis of identity. Saari has written of psychological health as the achievement of a complex identity which serves as a basis for a person perceiving and choosing behaviors. Identity is understood as a personal meaning system and involves the person's theory about self, the world, and the relationship between the self and the world and the world and the self.[15] Additionally, she sees pathology as a problem in the person's ability to create meaning which has as its foundation human relationships. Boundaries assist us in achieving a complex identity of self and other. When they are too open or too closed, they handicap our ability to realize deeper meaning in relationships.

Crisis of Identity

Our problem is that we have assumed a "truncated identity" because we have limited the depth of our relationships with others to superficial narratives. Too often we no longer have the depth to sustain us, especially in difficult and tumultuous times. We can be weak anorexia skeletons of soulless Christians clinging to others for identity or isolated in our fearfulness of being close to something of depth. Either of these can precipitate a crisis of identity.

There are many avenues to a crisis of identity. The various chapter topics of this book may be the origin of a crisis of identity. When our life order is too threatened or too disturbed we may face a crisis of identity. Our basic integration of the self may be torn apart in such circumstances. Here again, the trauma victim is an example of this. The person who has been severely abused as a child will sometimes split off part of the self and have a lack of integration of personhood. The most profound crisis of identity may be found in the persons with multiple personality disorder (now called Dissociative Identity Disorder). They are so fragmented that they have split off or dissociated parts of themselves which become distinct personalities. Often some of the personalities even take on the personality characteristics of abusers from the person's past, thus setting up a war within the person. There is no integrated whole.

While none of us are totally integrated, to have some integration is necessary for us to have a sense of self and self-identity. Integration gives congruence between what we believe and how we live. It provides coherence and stability. While none of us experience this in a perfect way, it is vital for our identity formation.

> Life must somehow make sense. Connections must be made. Meanings must be found that link together both the random and the regular events that have occurred to give them a quality of predictability and wholeness. To be without such a structure of interpretation is to find oneself threatened with chaos and profound anxiety. . . .[16]

Responses to a Crisis of Identity

Kao gives three possible responses to an identity crisis which he states comes again and again in adulthood:

1. to become closed to the new environment by reinforcing the old identity;
2. to be so totally overwhelmed by the new environment that he or she suffers from identity diffusion or confusion; and
3. to be open enough to the new challenge while maintaining one's internal integration in the process of identity reformation.[17]

To be able to integrate and not be overwhelmed requires a basic foundation from which to incorporate the crisis. The extent of the crisis can be determined by the severity of the event or situation one is facing and other factors, in addition to this foundation. A person's ability to incorporate certain internal principles and beliefs into a spiritual core can be a major factor in how a crisis of personal identity is faced and resolved.

The Need of a Spiritual Core

James Hillman has written about a concept he calls the acorn theory to describe that "which holds that each person bears a uniqueness that asks to be lived and that is already present before it can be lived."[18] He bases this upon the concept from Plato that each person comes into the world with a special calling. He sees this lack of destiny and personal calling as one of the reasons for meaninglessness. Although Hillman is not attempting to connect this to Christianity, it has been a concept that has not only been lost to modern humanity, it is far too often lost in the church. However, it certainly has an essential history in Christian teachings.

The historical teaching of Christianity has been that we are created in the image of God. Christianity has taught that there is a Divine spark in each person. Additionally, the teaching that God suffered in Christ to offer redemption has elevated the worth of the person to a child of God. "The classical error of historical Christianity is that we have never started with the value of the person. Rather, we have started with the 'unworthiness of the sinner' and that starting point has set the stage for the glorification of human shame in Christian theology."[19] Redemptive history is the basis for the Christian realizing the enormous worth of each person and the identity we each have in the Christ event. "Identity, considered theologically, thus implies calling and intentionality as well as destiny and roots."[20] Figure 13.1 (Chapter 13) suggests that redemptive history assists in answering some of the vital questions of life including those pertaining to identity.

Kao states, "It is evident that identity refers to the quality which signifies a person's uniqueness, individuality, specificity, and idiosyncrasy. At the same time, identity has the quality of the continuously tested sameness in the process of dynamic changes in one's interaction with his environment. It gives answers to the question of "who am I?"[21] He goes on to connect this sameness to eternity and the faithfulness of the Ultimate Being that gives firmness to life and prevents internal total disintegration.

Kass has found that spiritual experiences are associated with persons having life purpose and satisfaction and being associated with decreases in frequency of stress-related medical problems.[22] He refers to Tillich's "ontological insecurity" (a perception that meaning is lacking in life and God does not exist) and gives a converse term "ontological harmony" that describes a worldview that reduces anxiety and provides more meaning even in stressful situations due to a belief in God or a Ground of Being, to use Tillich's term. Kass states, "our culture's failure to recognize the value of an internally focused perceptual orientation may be denying many individuals an important health-promoting resource: the experience of our spiritual core.[23]

The spiritual core assists us in dealing with our crisis of identity. The spiritual core consists of a sense of calling and connection, worth and destiny, meaning and purpose that have a sense of transcendence about them. This flows from a connection to an "I am" which is much bigger than the "I." Narramore states, "Ultimately a solid source of identity comes from knowing who one is in the eyes of the creator!"[24] Identity is always a product of relationship and identity fails to exist where there is no relationship.[25] It is not achievement or performance based but is given in grace. It is this gospel that communicates a profound sense of worth and dignity to each individual. The relationship with God through the redemptive event of Christ reveals clearly this worth and dignity. Our worth does not have to be based upon the "god of the bottom line."[26] The god of the bottom line is what is so prevalent in our society and it renders judgment without mercy to those who do not perform and produce to the satisfaction of the culture or the business. The bottom line is a powerful metaphor to focus our attention on the fact that we are judged in business by results."[27]

The good news in redemptive history is that we can be accepted in spite of our failures and faults. This provides fertile soil out of which our identities can grow, knowing we are accepted and valued. "Next to physical survival, the greatest need of a human being is psychological survival—to be understood, to be affirmed, to be validated, to be appreciated."[28] A more positive identity formation based on the story of redemptive history and the acceptance in the gospel provides competence based identifications for personal growth and development. "So then you are no longer strangers and sojourners, but you are fellow citizens with the saints and members of the household of God."[29]

Questions for Discussion/Reflection

1. Do you think there is a crisis of identity in our society? Why or why not?
2. How is an identity formed?
3. Does identity evolve and transform or does it usually remain fairly stable over time?
4. Has the church contributed to codependent or contradependent behavior? Has the church assisted in the balance of interdependence?
5. How does redemptive history relate to identity?

Chapter 13

The Crisis of Ethics

Lillian Rubin echoed a current topic of many when she titled one of her book chapters on working class families "People don't know right from wrong anymore."[1] She wrote of the yearning among these families for the absolutes of the past. In our postmodern society the norms of behavior are certainly more ambiguous than a few decades ago. The congruence between norms and actual behavior was not as solid as some might wish to believe for that era, but currently norms and behavior appear to be out of control. Who is the authority for correct behavior? Where do we find answers to our moral and ethical dilemmas? Carl Braaten has written that we live in a world that has been:

> flattened into facts without values, quantities without quality, broken up into bits and pieces without a whole, a body without a soul, mammon without mystery, a drama without a plot, a life without a future, sex without love, religion without faith, words without meaning.[2]

THE CRISIS OF ETHICS AND FUNDAMENTALISM

One crisis we are facing is the crisis of ethics. The response by some to the crisis of ethics in our postmodern society is a move toward fundamentalism. They are bombarded by a culture that appears out of control and they seek clear answers which can define right and wrong and give direction. Fundamentalism provides a way to preserve the traditional, thus preserving the traditional identity. One psychiatrist presents a summary of character-istics of some fundamentalists and fanatics in three areas:[3]

1. *Fear:* this includes fear of freedom which can result in dogmatism and conformism, fear of uncertainty which can result in the suppression of doubt, fear of conscience which can result in consciences that are excessively harsh, and fear of instincts which can result in denials of parts of themselves.
2. *Love:* This includes the common denial of love and replacing it with self-hate and hatred of others; there can be the development of group narcissism which includes a contempt for others outside the group.
3. *Knowledge:* This often includes a rigidity and lack of openness, very dense filters to any new information, opposition of questioning, a legalistic approach to morality, and an anti-intellectualism.

Many sincere persons travel through a form of fundamentalism at some point in their religious journies. The structure of fundamentalism provides needed boundaries for some in times of crisis and transition. While there is, of course, danger in some of the extremes of fundamentalism, many fundamentalists "are basically good people who have big problems, or cause problems only if their faith is threatened by internal or external factors."[4] One of the main problems I see with a more fundamentalist approach is that it places rules and dogma over relationship. This was a problem in the days of Christ and continues across various parts of the world.

A FOUNDATION FOR THE ETHICS OF LIFE

The New Testament approach appears to me to be a good place to look for a foundation for ethics for its appeal is toward the priority of principles and relationships rather than to any black and white simplistic approach. In this chapter we will only address the foundation of ethics which, particularly, for Christians grows out of redemptive history. In fact, redemptive history and the central focus of the Christ event is the basis for many important motivations, answers, and understandings as illustrated in Figure 13.1. The Christian story of redemptive history can assist us as we struggle with questions of living such as: Identity: "Who am I?"; Relationship: "How am I accepted?"; and "How should I accept others?"; Community: "Where do I belong?" as well as the emphasis of this chapter, Ethics: "How shall I live?"

Narrative Theology and Narrative Therapy

In recent decades there has appeared on the theological scene a movement called story or narrative theology. While certainly not

FIGURE 13.1. The Impact of Redemptive History (The Christian Story)

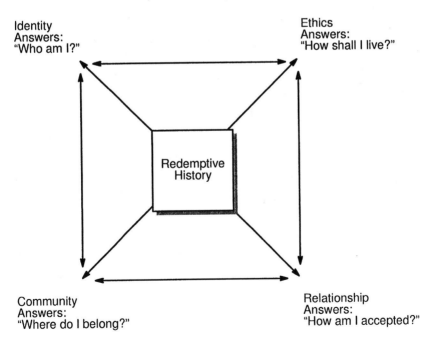

Identity
Answers:
"Who am I?"

Ethics
Answers:
"How shall I live?"

Redemptive
History

Community
Answers:
"Where do I belong?"

Relationship
Answers:
"How am I accepted?"

answering all our problems in finding ethics to live by, I believe story theology has some important characteristics. Also in the area of therapy we now have what is called narrative therapy. While I cannot do justice to these to these disciplines and I will probably distort them to some degree, I would like to use them to emphasize some guideline in the area of ethics.

We all have personal stories. These can be confining and stifling as when something that should be "merely a prism of the mind"[5] becomes a prison of the mind. On the other hand, stories can be liberating and expanding. One deficit among many in our postmodern society is that they do not have positive stories which give life direction. In our multimedia age we often no longer listen to oral traditions from our families, communities, and churches. This appears to me to lead to fragmentation and lack of commitment. We do not have a foundation from which to define our lives. Some have only the influence of television or the inner city gang to define who they are. We are lacking in living theology and story as we find in persons such as Mother Teresa. Therefore, our ethics suffer from lack of nourishment and vitality. In the interest of securing a rational foundation for morality, contemporary ethical theory has ignored or rejected the significance of narrative.[6]

Story theology emphasizes the centrality of story in the scriptures as opposed to other theological approaches where story can be lost.[7] It seeks to recapture the ancient method of storytelling that was the experience of both Jewish and Christian traditions.[8]

> stories appeal to the imagination, to the place within us where our images of reality, life, and ourselves reside. The great stories of the Bible image what religious life is all about.[9]

An example of this for the people of Israel is the story about being led out of Egypt, the exodus story. The people of Israel were slaves in Egypt when God brought liberation through Moses. This story was often repeated and was a call for Israel to respond to the greatness of God and it gave them an identity as being valued by God's participation in their lives. Such stories are numerous in the scriptures and the ultimate story unfolds for the Christian in the New Testament with the story of Jesus Christ. Jesus himself was a storyteller, especially in his parables. Even in the writings of the apostle Paul we could state that his ethics are based or founded upon story. In several of the Pauline epistles the authors first sketch out the theology or the story of Christ then later call to ethical behavior based on the story of Christ.

> The authority of scripture derives its intelligibility from the existence of a community that knows its life depends on faithful remembering of God's care of his creation through the calling of Israel and the life of Jesus. . . . The Bible does not so much provide a morality as it is the source of images and analogues that help us understand and interpret the nature of our existence.[10]

For me the theology of the New Testament fits appropriately in a postmodern age for it looks at broader strokes than legalism provides. "Modernist thinkers tend to be concerned with facts and rules, postmodernists are concerned with meaning. In their search for and examination of meaning, postmodernists find metaphors from the humanities more useful than modernists the metaphors of nineteenth-century science."[11]

The realities we experience are brought forth by our stories and "are then kept alive and passed along in the stories that we live and tell."[12] We make sense of, organize, and define our worlds by the stories we tell and believe.

Some have criticized postmodernism as being moral relativism, but this does not have to be the case.

> When we say that there are many possible stories about self (or about other aspects of reality), we do not mean to say that "anything goes." Rather, we are motivated to examine

our constructions and stories—how they have come to be and what their effects are on our selves and others."[13]

While there is less emphasis on rules and authoritative claims in a postmodern approach, there is on the other hand a greater realization of the context and particular situation. While anything can be taken to extremes and certainly this could be said of many modern approaches as well, postmodernism's focus on the unique-ness of each person and situation brings a sometimes neglected aspect to ethical considerations. While the term postmodernism is used in many ways: "In general, postmodernism is antimodern and sees the enlightenment with its emphasis that reason and science leads us along a linear path toward unerring progress, as a failed project. . . . Postmodernism questions authority and challenges the status quo."[14]

While postmodernism is often lacking in value judgments and ethical foundations at one level, its respect for context and the unique understanding of each person is very ethical on a meta-level. While I am borrowing the part of postmodernism that I want and not accepting it completely (something some would say is impossible to do), I find it very helpful when put against the template of the method of Christ. In many ways key ideas of postmodernism are very close to His teaching and manner of relating.

There are examples of Jesus taking a much wider approach than the people of his day. In many ways he deconstructed his society. An example is the consideration of helping persons on the Sabbath or eating grain on the Sabbath. Jesus upset hierarchy. He opposed the status quo. He "spoke as one having authority" yet his authority was completely different from the hierarchical authority of his day. He rebelled against limited interpretations and understandings.

We must say that the Bible has no independent interest in ethics . . . the Bible is not an ethical manual any more than it is a systematic theology. The Bible is written as history. It is a story of God's redemptive acts. Biblical ethics are not artificially attached to this story. They are embedded in the story itself. These ethical principles are not little gold nuggets which must be dug out of solid rock so they can be melted down together. In this respect Judeo-Christian ethics are absolutely unique.[15]

Those who formulate a legalist law-based approach to ethics do so by detaching the gospel from Christianity. Our Western culture easily becomes myopic with an overemphasis on law or cheap grace as a means of simplifying, but this is done as perversion of the gospel. I believe ethics must always flow from love and faith. "The New Testament provides a compass, but not a map. The compass is the mercy of Christ manifest to us sinners on Calvary."[16]

In keeping with our focus on the importance of relationship, it is our contention that relationship can be a basis for ethical behavior. For the Christian it is not some legalist following of a code, but living in relationship and as a response to the person, Christ.

In the New Testament:

> it is clear that the apostles constantly reason from what God has done for us in Christ to how we ought to live. The central commandment of our Lord is that we ought to love one another *as* he has loved us. . . . There are, of course, some concrete instructions and commandments in the New Testament, but these are neither the sum nor the center of Christian ethics. . . . The Christian's supreme Law is not a code but a Person.[17]

Christian ethics are thus based upon this Person and the story that we refer to as the gospel.[18] I have known those who have been extremely orthodox according to their church's view, and kept the outward standards of the church, but in their hearts had a negative personal story. Therefore, they were some of the most intolerant and heartless people I have ever known. We must be compassionate toward such persons, but I found the description of one author rather accurate: "They are like dried-up old prunes with a distorted view of life, no sense of humor and a bad conscience."[19] I believe such persons often have a negative life story which then becomes the lens through which they use their religion. The lens distorts and blurs the beauty of the gospel and perverts Christian ethics.

We can be very orthodox, very governed by rules and technical theology and yet miss the essence of being guided by the story of the Christ event. So often we then attempt to answer questions no one is asking and miss the hurts and real questions of those around us. This to me is the worse distortion of ethics. The Christian story calls for a broader base for living, one not consumed with such perfection, but instead motivated by the story of love and forgiveness. The story of the good Samaritan taught by Christ illustrates this well:

> A man was going down from Jerusalem to Jericho, when he fell into the hands of robbers. They stripped him of his clothes, beat him and went away, leaving him half dead. A priest happened to be going down the same road, and when he saw the man, he passed by on the other side. So, too, a Levite, when he came to the place and saw him, passed by on the other side. But a Samaritan, as he traveled, came where the man was and when he saw him, he took pity on him. He went to him and bandaged his wounds, pouring on oil and wine. Then he put him on his own donkey, took him to an inn and took care of him. The next day he took out two silver coins and gave them to the innkeeper. "Look after him," he said, "and when I return I will reimburse you for any extra expense you may have." Which of these three do you think was a neighbor to the man who fell into the hands of robbers? The expert in the law replied, "The one who had mercy on him." Jesus told him, "Go and do likewise."[20]

We must remember that this powerful story was told to persons who considered the priest and Levite to be among the righteous and the Samaritans to be outcasts. Note that the technical theological experts of the time do not show mercy in the story. The expert of the law who at the end answered the question of Christ could not even bring himself to say the word Samaritan in his answer. "The good Samaritan's theology was not as technically correct as the theology of the priest or Levite, but the spirit of his religion was far more in harmony with the spirit of heaven."[21] Here we have an interesting paradox of those who were the formal ethicists, those who spent their lives deciding what was or was not proper behavior, being the most unethical of all!

Therefore, we cannot propose that more laws, rules, orthodoxy, technical expertise, or moral theories are what is most needed. These all have their place as guidelines, but they cannot change and motivate the heart. They can be cold and lifeless. Stories, on the other hand, touch our intellect as well as our emotions. Stories approach us in a much more integrated fashion. For Christians the Christ event or story calls us to live ethically in response to what Christ has done. Or as I heard Stephen Sprinkle of Brite Divinity School put it: "The Christian life doesn't have an ethic it *is an ethic*." The Christian life is not a response to a code of rules or laws, but as stated above is a response to Christ and a relationship with Him. This calls for a radical ethic.

Questions for Discussion/Reflection

1. What ethics do you live by? Is there a particular organization to your ethics?
2. How much of our ethics are culturally bound?
3. What stories have influenced your ethics?
4. Can we have common ethics in a pluralistic society?
5. How does the redemptive story impact upon your ethics?

Chapter 14

The Crisis of Working
with People in Crisis

Dr. Charles Figley, a professor at Florida State University, has coined the term "compassion fatigue" to describe the effect of working in the helping professions.[1] There is a process of depleting the energy of the helper that occurs over time when assisting others, especially those who have been traumatized. Therefore, before ending this book we must briefly address this type of crisis in the life of the helper or counselor.

This chapter presents some basic processes for restoring and replenishing the life as the counselor or helper works with persons in crisis. The main theme is that the balanced spirituality mentioned in Chapter 10 can make a critical difference for many once energetic counselors who are now suffering from disillusionment or burnout and can be protective for those entering the field.

Nelson Thayer defines spirituality as the human capacity to experience, be conscious of, and relate to a dimension of power and meaning beyond the world of our immediate senses.[2] This concept of spirituality can help provide the needed strength to deal with the wear and tear of helping others in crisis. Charles Whitfield describes spirituality as a divine consciousness within each person which is a sanctuary from stress.[3] In the Christian

---

The original version of this chapter appeared as "Preventing Burnout Through Spirituality" in *The Counselor,* Volume 9, No. 3, 1991. Used by permission.

tradition this involves a relationship with Christ. In particular, a spiritual life can help one to have a greater sense of transcendence, solitude, discipline, and community.

FINDING MEANING IN LIFE

The existential therapist, Rollo May, believes that counselors should be concerned with helping others discover meaning and "problems of being" rather than with problem solving only. He and other existential writers and therapists can help us understand transcendence.

The concept of spirituality can help individuals find and maintain meaning in life. This purpose may be found by transcending the individual self as in the belief in God or a higher power or by descending to a place deep within each being.

Far too often counselors and helpers get caught up in the immediate crisis and fail to look at the larger issues of life. This occurs in the professional and lay involvement with those in crisis as well as in personal experiences. On the other hand, Heidegger wrote that individuals should not think of themselves as being apart from the world.[4] There must be a balance.

However, in order not to be overwhelmed, helpers need to realize the freedom to choose personal attitudes in any given situation. This is vital according to Victor Frankl who was able to survive the concentration camps due to his ability to find a way to choose even in the midst of severe external control and abuse.[5] This human freedom can assist helpers in transcending the limitations of the present crisis, whether personal or at the time of assisting others. It gives the individual a broader basis for finding meaning in life. There is a purpose in believing in the concept of God or a higher power that presents a reality and meaning in life beyond the immediate senses.

Paul Tillich wrote that individuals need to have the courage to "live from the inside."[6] A deep experience of transcendence can help achieve this when the pressures of life are too great. Individuals can relate differently if they are able to be in touch with the immediate situation, yet look beyond it to other potentialities.

FINDING SANCTUARY

Closely related to the concept of inner transcendence is that of solitude. As mentioned above, Dr. Whitfield sees the "higher self" as an important place to retreat to or stay in touch with as counselors or helpers. Many people do not reach out until they have "bottomed out" in their lives. Many who ask for help are only beginning to face extremely stressful situations that have precipitated a crisis for them. If the only self we are in contact with is the self that is relating to the disastrous event or condition, it is no wonder that many in the helping fields experience burnout. We all need to have a place or a community of solitude in which we can replenish personal vitality and energy.

Such a place may be inside or outside of the personal self. Mystics and spiritual pilgrims throughout history have found retreats of solitude necessary to keep them in contact with their spirituality. These sanctuaries can be churches or temples; they can also be places incorporating the beauty and peace of nature. For some it is a community of support, acceptance, and freedom to be oneself.

A spiritual quality is found in taking a walk in the woods when the aloneness is connected with nature. Just as the counseling room is a safe sanctuary for clients, counselors too need a sanctuary where there is solitude to find the inner peace uninterrupted by stress and commotion.

LEARN TO SURRENDER

Counselors and pastors sometimes speak of resistant persons who have not learned how to surrender. However, counselors also have this problem. Caregivers are not all powerful and cannot help clients solve all their problems. Some caregivers come into the profession with a "Messiah Complex," where they believe they can save persons from past traumas, present problems, and future difficulties. It is important to be optimistic, but also to be realistic. We may be an instrument of salvation, but salvation does not come from us. If counselors even adjust to deal with some of their messiah complex while continuing to believe a large part of it, it can be detrimental. This can cause burnout since counselors fall into the trap of codependency with clients. Thus each time the client fails, so too does the counselor.

Carl Jung wrote of the prototype of treatment as being the confessional.[7] Perhaps counselors need to confess to their God or higher power and to other trusted co-workers their lack of surrender. This might be good treatment for counselors who "white knuckle" it too often and, therefore, waste energy to fool themselves.

A SENSE OF DISCIPLINE

Too often today we ignore the discipline involved in spirituality. Kenneth Mitchell has written of the danger of using spirituality as a catchall word. Rather, it is useful for persons as "a disciplined, principled set of patterns of habits . . . for the purpose of grounding their ordinary lives."[8]

Balanced spirituality requires some form of discipline, even if it is simply scheduling a walk in nature. It also requires discipline to find the inner self and to transcend the limits of the present situation. Many have incorporated some type of "centering" or meditation as a spiritual discipline. Meditation can be defined as a listening to God and to ourselves. The discipline is not in the working at it; rather it comes in the surrender of it. Rather than thinking of the split between the psyche and the body (soma) that is so common in Western thought, we should think of "wholeness," where being in touch with the inner self is being in touch with the whole being. This may include the need for more balanced diet, exercise, and rest.

Counselors also need to be disciplined by having other interests besides counseling and reading about counseling. A narrow focus on life does not take into consideration the vastness of the spiritual being. Discipline that aids counselors in addressing the whole being can be a very important safeguard against compassion fatigue.

INCORPORATING OTHERS

Many in the helping professions are both lonely and alone. Research has shown that children of psychotherapists often see their parents as exceptionally lonely and socially ostracized.[9] A minister who was feeling burnout wrote the following in a paper for a class I taught:

> Ministers generally feel a great deal of loneliness. We get little support or encouragement. . . . Many of us reach a point where there is nothing left to give.

It is no longer a secret that many in the ministry state that ministry has had a negative impact on their personal and family lives. An unrealistic pressure often occurs from the congregation or from inside the minister to be the ideal person or have the ideal family. This pressure leads to a facade that prevents sharing of the clergy person's own pains and struggles and isolates the minister even more.

There is an asymmetrical intimacy that exists in the therapeutic relationship where caregivers share very little of themselves while the persons they are assisting pour out the deepest pains of their souls. Being a caregiver can be an escape for some as they live vicariously through the feelings of others while avoiding personal issues. It can be a disaster if caregivers use the profession to escape personal feelings and relationships with others.

It is imperative for counselors to be in community and to be in relationships with others outside their client world. As spiritual beings, individuals need to belong to a community because it can magnify happiness and lessen pain. Several models of therapy emphasize this need, yet often counselors fail to recognize their own denied needs. Finding a place to belong, to be in community, and to experience connectedness should be a high priority for those in helping positions.

Spirituality adds to the caregiver's personal life which can mean the difference between finding meaning and satisfaction in a helping career or becoming a causality to compassion fatigue and spiritual crisis. The issue is for counselors to move past the denials and rationalizations and look at the needs of their personal lives as clearly as they have learned to look at the needs of those they are assisting.

Questions for Discussion/Reflection

1. What are some of the necessary balances to working with people in crisis?
2. Can a person be a caregiver without being codependent?
3. Some say those who are caregivers are working out their own problems by working with others. What do you think?
4. Why are caregivers burning out so often today?
5. How can communities of worship better emotionally support their caregivers?

Epilogue

We do not live in this world for very long without the experience of crisis. We could define our very first experience of birth as a crisis, although it is also a natural stage of development. As we mature we develop understandings and beliefs about the world that become susceptible to change. Change can be gradual or dramatic, something assimilated and accommodated, or something that is overwhelming and traumatizing. Certain change initiates a crisis of meaning as assumptions previously held are challenged, shaken, or even destroyed. As outlined in the preceding chapters, such contexts and experiences are often the wombs from which spiritual crises come forth.

The good news is, and the biblical themes teach, in the midst of chaos there is creation, in the midst of darkness a light appears, in the midst of death there is resurrection, in the midst the brokenness there is a new life, in the midst of a crooked way there is a straight path, and in the midst of a world self-destructing there is a new earth. One of the great Christian beliefs is: everything is not as it appears. The old axiom that crisis provides opportunity is ever true even when it does not yet reveal itself. During crisis the narrowing of perspectives can extremely limit us. We can be stuck in our inability to take risks. We can be blinded by our present circumstances. We can feel all alone. Facing the spiritual aspects of crisis can widen our perspectives, move us to creative risks, open our experience to greater possibilities, and connect us to resources beyond ourselves. This does not remove all the uncertainty from life, numb every pain of living, nor solve all the ambiguities of existence. However, I believe being true to our spiritual selves provides the greatest opportunity for growth in the midst of the crises of our lives. Assisting others in this spiritual journey by listening, accepting, and asking the larger existential questions is a most potent medicine for healing.

If crisis so often brings forth spiritual and existential issues as I have suggested in this book, we must use sensitive, appropriate, and caring ways to address these aspects of the crisis experience. Thus, we will truly help others and ourselves survive trauma to the soul.

Notes

Chapter 1

1. Engles, G., The Need for a New Medical Model, *Science,* 1977, 196, pp. 129-136.
2. Covey, S., Merrill, A., Merrill, R., *First Things First,* New York: Simon and Schuster, Fireside Edition, 1995. Covey does better at seeking an integration of these than most. He also applies the concept of synergism to them which I have found helpful.
3. Job 42:3.*
4. Friedman, E., *Generation to Generation,* New York: The Guilford Press, 1985, p. 5.

Chapter 2

1. Wiesel, E., *Night.* New York: Hill and Wang, 1960, p. ix.
2. Brende, J., Post-Traumatic Spiritual Alienation and Recovery in Vietnam Combat Veterans. *Spirituality Today,* 1989, 41, p. 325.
3. Mahedy, P., *Out of The Night: The Spiritual Journey of Vietnam Vets.* New York: Ballantine, 1986, p. 32.
4. Baker, I., Lecture: *The Father Archetype,* The Jungian Winter Institute, Switzerland, 1989.
5. van der Kolk, B., The Trauma Spectrum: The Interaction of Biological and Social Events in the Genesis of the Trauma Response. *The Journal of Traumatic Stress,* 1988, 1, 5, pp. 273-290.
6. Mahedy, *op. cit.,* p. 208.
7. Sinclair, N., *Horrific Traumata.* Binghamton, NY: The Haworth Press, 1993.
8. American Psychiatric Association: *Diagnostic and Statistical Manual of Mental Disorders,* Fourth Edition. Washington, DC: American Psychiatric Press, 1994.
9. van der Kolk, B. (Ed.)., The Psychological Consequences of Overwhelming Life Experiences. *Psychological Trauma,* Washington, DC: Psychiatric Press, 1987, pp. 2-3.

---

*Citations from the Bible are from the New International Version unless otherwise indicated.

10. Sinclair, *op. cit.,* p. 65.

11. Brende, J., *Overcoming Trauma and Stress, Biblical Teaching About Traumatic Experiences and Recovery.* Columbus, GA: Trauma Recovery Publications, 1993.

12. Sinclair, *op. cit.,* p. 45.

13. St. Clair, M., *Object Relations and Self Psychology.* Monterey, CA: Brooks/Cole, 1986.

14. Moore, T., *Care of the Soul.* New York: Harper Collins, 1992, p. 5.

15. Whitfield, C., *Alcoholism, Attachments, and Spirituality.* New York: Perrin, 1985.

16. Booth, L., *Breaking the Chains: Understanding Religious Addiction and Religious Abuse.* Long Beach: Emmaus Publications, 1989.

17. Bradshaw, J., *Healing the Shame that Binds You.* Dearfield Beach, FL, Health Communications, Inc., 1988.

18. Masterson, J. and Klein, R. (eds.), *Psychotherapy of the Disorders of the Self.* New York: Brunner/Mazel, 1989.

19. Brende, *op. cit.,* 1989.

20. Spiegel, D., Dissociating Damage. *American Journal of Clinical Hypnosis,* 1986, 29, p. 124.

21. Jung, C., *Modern Man in Search of a Soul.* New York: Harcourt Jovanovich, 1933.

22. Pynoos R., Traumatic Stress and Developmental Psychopathology in Children and Adolescents. In John Oldham, Michelle Riba, and Allan Tasman (eds.) *Review of Psychiatry,* 1993, 12, p. 222.

23. Marmar, C., Foy, D., Kagan, B., and Pyroos, R., An Integrated Approach for Treating Posttraumatic Stress. In John Oldham, Michelle Riba, and Alban Tasman (eds.) *Review of Psychiatry,* 1993, 12, pp. 239-272.

24. McBride, J., Mistaking Religion for Spirituality, *The Pastoral Forum.* Spring, 1990, 9, 1, pp. 10-11.

25. Solomon, M., *Narcissism and Intimacy.* New York: W.W. Norton & Co., 1989, p. 12.

26. van der Kolk, B. (ed.), *Post-Traumatic Stress Disorder: Psychological and Biological Sequelae.* Washington, DC: American Psychological Press, Inc., 1984, p. 5.

27. Armstrong, G., and Sinclair, N.D., Long-Term Outpatient Group Psychotherapy with Adult Survivors of Trauma. *The Pastoral Forum,* 9,2, 1990.

28. Herman, J.H., *Father-Daughter Incest.* Cambridge: Harvard University Press, 1981.

29. Estes, C.P., *Women Who Run with the Wolves.* New York: Ballantine Books, 1992, p. 383.

30. Armstrong and Sinclair, *op. cit.,* p. 238.

31. Estes, *op. cit.,* p. 383.

32. Moore, *op. cit.,* p. 238.

33. Kaplan, L.J., *Oneness and Separateness from Infant to Individual.* New York: Simon and Schuster, 1978.

34. Krystal, H., Psychoanalytic Views on Human Emotional Damages, in van der Kolk, Bessel (ed.), *Post-Traumatic Stress Disorder: Psychological and Biological Sequelae.* Washington, DC: American Psychological Press, 1984.

35. Jung, C. *op. cit.*

36. Bradshaw, *op. cit.,* p. 219.

37. Pearsall, P., *Making Miracles.* New York: Prentice Hall Press, 1991.

38. *Ibid.*

39. Yalom, I., *Love's Executioner.* New York: Basic Books, Inc., 1989.

40. Estes, *op. cit.,* pp. 377-378.

41. Psalms 23:4.

Chapter 3

1. Covey, S., *Seven Habits of Highly Effective People.* New York: Simon and Schuster, Fireside Edition, 1990, p. 96.

2. Griffith, J., and Griffith, M., Therapeutic Change in Religious Families: Working with the God-Construct. In Laurel Burton, (ed.), *Religion and the Family: When God Helps,* Binghamton, NY: The Haworth Press, 1992, pp. 63-86.

3. Howe, L., Crisis of Belief: An Object Relations Perspective. *The Journal of Pastoral Care,* 1990, 44, 1, pp. 42-53.

4. Cooper, T., The Psychotherapeutic Evangelism of John Bradshaw. *Pastoral Psychology,* 1995, 44, 2, p. 78.

5. Rinsley, D., *Developmental Pathogenesis and Treatment in Narcissistic Personalities,* Northdale, NJ: Jason Aronson, Inc., 1989, p. 4.

6. Luepnitz, D., *The Family Interpreted.* New York: Basic Books, Inc., 1988.

7. Fairbairn, W., *An Object Relations Theory of the Personality.* New York: Basic Books, Inc., 1952.

8. White, S., Imago Dei and Object Relations Theory: Implications for a Model of Human Development. *Journal of Psychology and Theology,* 12, 4, 1984, pp. 286-293.

9. Luepnitz, *op. cit.*

10. Horner, A., *Psychoanalytic Object Relations Theory.* Northvale, NJ: Jason Aronson, 1991, p. 8.

11. Richard, R., Differentiation of Self as a Therapeutic Goal for the Systemic Pastoral Counselor, *Journal of Pastoral Psychology,* 1, 1, 1987.

12. Kaplan, K. *Oneness and Separation: From Infant to Adult.* New York: Simon and Schuster, 1978, pp, 30, 31.

13. Horner, *op. cit.*

14. Framo, J., The Integration of Marital Therapy with Sessions with Family of Origin. In Alan Gurman and David Kniskern (eds.), *Handbook of Family Therapy,* New York: Brunner/Mazel, Inc., 1981, pp. 133-158.

15. Napier, A., *The Fragile Bond.* New York: Harper and Row, 1988, p. 16.

16. Solomon, M. *Narcissism and Intimacy.* New York: W.W. Norton & Co., Inc., 1989, p. 28.

17. Blanck, B., and Blanck, G., *Marriage and Personal Development.* New York: Columbia University Press, 1968.

18. Balswick, J., and Balswick, J., A Theological Basis for Family Relationships. *Journal of Psychology and Christianity,* 6, 3, 1987, pp. 37-49. Permission obtained to use model.

19. Chartier, M. Parenting: A Theological Model, *Journal of Psychology and Theology,* 5, 1978, pp. 54-61. Quoted in Balswick and Balswick.

20. McLean, S., The Language of Covenant and a Theology of the Family. *Consultation on a Theology of the Family,* Fuller Theological Seminary, 1984. Quoted in Balswick and Balswick.

21. Balswick, *op. cit.*

22. *Ibid.*

23. *Ibid.*

24. *Ibid.,* p. 44.

25. *Ibid.,* pp. 44, 45.

26. *Ibid.,* p. 47.

27. Jung, C., The Practice of Psychotherapy: Essays on the Psychology of the Transference and Other Subjects. In Herbert Read, Michael Fordham, and Gerhard Adler (eds.), *The Collected Works of C.G. Jung,* Translated by R.F.C. Hall, New York: Pantheon Books, 16, 1954, p. 243.

28. Crowther, C., and Stone, G., *Intimacy.* New York: Dell Publishing Company, 1986, p. 18.

29. Wynne, L., and Wynne, A., The Quest for Intimacy. *Journal of Marriage and Family Therapy,* 12, 4, 1986, pp. 384-394.

30. Balswick, *op. cit.*

31. Patterson, J., and Garwick, A., Levels of Meaning in Family Stress Theory. *Family Process,* 33, 3, 1994, pp. 287-304.

32. Hill, R., Generic Features of Families Under Stress, *Social Casework,* 49, 1958, pp. 139-150.

33. McCubbin, H., and Patterson, J., The Family Stress Process: The Double ABCX Model of Adjustment and Adaptation. In H. McCubbin and J. Patterson (eds.), *Advances and Developments in Family Stress Theory and Research,* Binghamton, NY: The Haworth Press, 1983, pp. 7-37.

34. *Ibid.*

35. Mullen, P., and Hill, W., A Family Systems Model for Pastoral Care and Counseling in Times of Crisis, *The Journal of Pastoral Care,* 64, 3, 1990.

Chapter 4

1. van Rooyen, S., Is the Church a Hole in the Head? *Unraveling Some Ideas,* Auburn, CA: Good News Unlimited, 1983, pp. 17-24.

2. Stokes, K., *Faith Is a Verb: Dynamics of Adult Faith Development.* Mystic, CT: Twenty-Third Publications, 1989.

3. Wilke, R., *And Are We Yet Alive?* Nashville, Abington, 1986, p. 9.

4. Brown, R., *The Significance of the Church.* Philadelphia: Westminster Press, MCMLVI, p. 17.

5. Achtemeier, P., *The Quest for Unity in the New Testament Church.* Philadelphia: Fortress Press, 1987, p. 2.

6. Friedman, E., *Generation to Generation: Family Process in Church and Synagogue.* New York: Guilford Press, 1985, p. 203.

7. Brinsmead, R., The Downfall of Western Christianity. *The Christian Verdict,* 1983, Essay 8, pp. 5, 6.

8. Wesley, J., Catholic Spirit. Sermons on Several Occasions, *Wesley's Works,* Volume 5, Sermons, Volume 1, 1771, p. 499.

9. Watzlawick, P., Weakland, J., and Fish, R., *Change: Principles of Problem Formation and Problem Resolution,* New York: W.W. Norton, 1974.

10. Deschenes, P., and Rogers, M., A Systems View of Jesus As Change Agent. *Journal of Psychology and Christianity,* 9, 2, 1981, pp. 128-135.

11. *Ibid.,* p. 129.

12. Miller, Keith, *A Second Touch.* Waco, TX: Word Books, p. 108.

13. Matthew 23:27, 28.

14. Tournier, P., *A Place for You,* New York: Harper and Row, 1968.

15. Brinsmead, R., The Shape of the Future Church. *The Christian Verdict,* Essay Four, 1983, p. 5.

16. Nelson, W., *A Plan for Letting the Church Become the Family of God.* Chicago: The Department of Home Mission and Evangelism, Evangelical Covenant Church, 1973, p. 1.

17. Miller, K., *The Taste of New Wine.* Waco: Word Books, 1965, p. 22.

18. Romans 15:7.

19. Williams, C., God Is Not Codependent. *The Other Side,* July/August 1991, p. 19.

20. Larson, B., *No Longer Strangers.* Waco, TX: Word Books, 1971, p. 27.

21. Moltmann, J., *The Open Church: Invitation to a Messianic Lifestyle.* London: SCM Press, 1978.

22. *Ibid.,* p. 33.

23. *Ibid.,* p. 87.

24. *Ibid.,* p. 115.

25. Schuller, R., *Self-Esteem: The New Reformation.* Waco, TX: Word Books, 1983, p. 13.

Chapter 5

1. Mason, N., Before We Begin. *Good News for Adventists,* Auburn, CA: Good News Unlimited, 1985, p. 16.

2. Barra, D., Carlson, E., Maize, M., Murphy, W., O'Neal, B., Sarver, R., and Zinner, E., The Dark Night of the Spirit: Grief Following a Loss of Religious Identity. In Doka, K. and Morgan, J. (eds.), *Death and Spirituality,* Amityville, NY: Baywood, 1993, pp. 291-308.

3. American Psychiatric Association: *Diagnostic and Statistical Manual,* Fourth Edition. Washington, DC: American Psychiatric Association, 1994, p. 843.

4. Kuhn, T., *The Structure of Scientific Revolutions.* Second Edition, 1970, Chicago, University of Chicago Press.

5. Covey, L., *The Seven Habits of Highly Effective People.* New York: Simon & Schuster, Fireside Edition, 1989.

6. Sutherland, A., Worldframes and God-Talk in Trauma and Suffering. *Journal of Pastoral Care,* 49, 3, 1995, pp. 280-293.

7. William James, *Talks to Teachers.* New York: Random House, 1987, p. 159.

8. van Rooyen, S., Finding the Road Again. *Good News Unlimited,* Auburn, CA: Good News Unlimited, November 1982, p. 4.

9. Brueggemann, W., *The Message of the Psalms.* Minneapolis: Augsburg Fortress Press, 1984.

10. Lukoff, D., and Turner, R., Cultural Considerations in the Assessment and Treatment of Religious and Spiritual Problems. *Psychiatric Clinics,* 18, 3, 1995, pp. 467-486.

11. Rhodes, S., Conversion as Crisis and Process: A Comparison of Two Models. *Journal of Psychology and Christianity,* 5, 3, 1987, p. 22.

12. Rogers, J., Dissonance and Christian Formation, *Journal of Psychology and Christianity,* 11, 1, 1992, pp. 5-13.

13. Rogers, *Ibid.*

14. Matthew 12:24.

15. Flower, J., *Stages of Faith.* San Francisco: Harper and Row, 1981.

16. Rogers, *op. cit.,* p. 23.

17. Matthew 18:3.

18. Rhodes, *op. cit.,* p. 23.

19. Rhodes, *Ibid.,* p. 23.

20. Loder, J., *The Transforming Moment.* Second Edition, Colorado Springs, CO: Helmers and Howard, 1989, p. 229.

21. Rhodes, *op. cit.,* p. 26.

22. Sutherland, *op. cit.,* pp. 285-286.

23. *Faith Development in the Adult Life Cycle: The Report of a Research Project.* New Haven: Religious Research Center, 1987.

24. Sutherland, *op. cit.*

25. Stokes, K., *Faith Is a Verb: Dynamic of Adult Faith Development.* Mystic, CN: Twenty-Third Publications, 1989.

26. Brueggemann, W., Parks, S., and Groome, T., *To Act Justly, Love Tenderly, Walk Humbly: An Agenda for Ministers.* New York: Paulist Press, 1986.

Chapter 6

1. Quoted in: Stott, J., *Balanced Christianity.* Madison, WI: Inter-Varsity Press.

Chapter 7

1. Peck, S., *The Road Less Traveled.* New York: Simon and Schuester, Touchstone Edition, 1978.

2. Garner, R., The Art of Psychoanalysis: On Oscillation and Other Matters. *Journal of the American Psychoanalytic Association,* 34, 4, 1989, pp. 851-870.

3. Perry, W., *Forms of Intellectual and Ethical Development in the College Years—A Scheme.* New York: Holt, Reinhart, and Winston, 1970.

4. Linehan, M., *Cognitive-Behavioral Treatment of Borderline Personality Disorder.* New York: Guilford Press, 1993.

5. Lloyd, G., *Polarity and Analogy.* Cambridge: University Press, 1971.

6. McBride, J., and Arthur, G., Competing Polarities in Resident Life. *Annals of Behavioral Sciences and Medical Education,* 2, 2, 1995, pp. 93-98.

7. Brown, R., *Spirituality and Liberation.* 1988, Philadelphia: Westminster Press.

8. Watts, A., *The Two Hands of God: The Myths of Polarity.* 1963, New York: George Brazilles, Inc., p. 52.

9. Snodgrass, K., *Between Two Truths: Living with Biblical Tensions.* Grand Rapids: Zondervan, 1990, p. 35.

10. Zalaquett, C., The Internal Parts Model: Parts, Polarities, and Dichotomies. *Journal of Integrative and Eclectic Psychotherapy,* 8, 4, 1989, pp. 329-343.

11. Brown, *Ibid.,* p. 31.

12. Zalaquett, *op. cit.*

13. Linehan, *op. cit.,* p. 33.

14. Zalaquett, *op. cit.*

15. Linehan, *op. cit.*

16. Heath, D., Teaching for Adult Effectiveness. *Journal of Experiential Education,* 1, 1, 1978, pp. 6-11.

17. Zalaquett, *op. cit.*

18. *Ibid.*

19. Mason, N., Editorial, *Good News Unlimited,* Auburn, CA: Good News Unlimited, January, 1982, p. 2.

20. Tritt, D., Cognitions of Self as Learner: A Necessary Objective in Experiential Education. *Psychological Reports,* 69, 1991, pp. 591-598.

21. Zalaquett, *op. cit.*

22. *Ibid.*

23. James M., and Jongeward, D., *Born to Win.* Reading, MA: Addison-Westley, 1971, p. 9. Quoted in Zalaquett.

24. Zalaquett, *op. cit.,* p. 337.

25. *Ibid,* p. 28.

26. Snodgrass, *op. cit.,* p. 32.

27. Wolff-Salin, M., *No Other Light.* New York: The Crossroad Publishing Company, 1986, p. 60.

28. Snodgrass, *op. cit.*

29. Zalaquett, *op. cit.,* p. 337.

30. Snodgrass, *op. cit.,* pp. 187-189.

31. Wolff-Salin, *op. cit.,* p. 50.

Chapter 8

1. Wolterstorff, N., *Lament for a Son.* Grand Rapids: Eerdmans, 1987, pp. 31, 33, 68. Quoted in Eibner, R., On the Grief Journey: The Mystery of God and the Search for Meaning, *Pastoral Science,* 14, 1995, pp. 65-76.

2. Eibner, R., *On the Grief Journey: The Mystery of God and the Search for Meaning.* Pastoral Science, 14, 1995, pp. 65-76.

3. McDaniel, S., Campbell, T., and Seaburn, D., *Family-Oriented Primary Care.* New York: Springer-Verlag, 1990.

4. Bowlby, J., *Loss.* New York: Basic Books, 1980.

5. Wistow, F., Goodbye, *The Family Networker.* November-December, 1986, pp. 22-27.

6. Crosby, J., and Jose, N., Death: Family Adjustment to Loss. In Charles Figley and Hamilton, McCubbin (eds.), *Stress and the Family, Volume 2, Coping with Catastrophe,* New York: Brunner/Mazel, pp. 81-82.

7. Kübler-Ross, E., *On Death and Dying,* New York: Macmillan, 1969.

8. Reisz, F., A Dying Person is a Living Person. *The Journal of Pastoral Care,* 46, 2, 1992.

9. Bowlby, *op. cit.*

10. Shapiro, E., *Grief as a Family Process.* New York: Gilford Press, 1994.

11. Simon, R., Editorial, *The Family Networker,* January-February, 1996.

12. Eibner, *op. cit.,* p. 75.

13. Buber, M., *The Knowledge of Man.* Maurice Friedman (editor and translator), New York: Harper and Row, 1965, p. 70.

14. Matthew 25:30.

15. Marty, M., *A Cry of Absence: Reflections for the Winter of the Heart.* San Francisco: Harper and Row, 1983, p. 2.

16. Stone, H., Theodicy in Pastoral Counseling. *Journal of Pastoral Psychology,* 1987, 1, 1, pp. 47-62.

17. *Ibid.,* p. 50.

18. Beckman, R., Breaking Bad News—Why Is It Still So Difficult? *British Medical Journal,* 1984, 288, 1, pp. 1597-1599.

19. Gerkin, C., *Crisis Experience in Modern Life.* Nashville, TN: Abington Press, 1979, p. 104.

20. Streets, F., Bearing the Spirit Home. In Howard M. Spiro, Mary G. McCrea-Curmen, and Lee Palmer Wandel (eds.), *Facing Death: Where Culture, Religion, and Medicine Meet,* New Haven: Yale University Press, 1996, pp. 180-183.

21. Kübler-Ross, E., Braga, L., and Braga, O. In Elizabeth Kübler-Ross, Laurie Braga, and Joseph Braga, General Editors, *Death: The Final Stage of Growth,* New York: Simon & Schuster, Inc., Touchstone Edition, 1986, p. 167.

Chapter 9

1. The original version of this story first appeared in: McBride, J., A Biopsychosocial Existential Experience. *Georgia Association of Family Practice Journal,* 16, 4, 1995, p. 8. Used by permission.

2. Kleinman, A., *The Illness Narratives: Suffering, Healing, and the Human Condition.* New York: Basic Books.

3. Rolland, J., *Families, Illness, and Disability.* New York: Basic Books, 1994.

4. *Ibid.*

5. Kluckhohn, F., Variations in the Basic Values of Family Systems. In N.W. Bell and E.F. Vogel (eds.), *A Modern Introduction to the Family,* Glencoe, IL: The Free Press, 1960. Referred to in Rolland.

6. Pullin, I., and Kanaan, S., *Medical Crisis Counseling.* New York: W.W. Norton Company.

7. Leahey, M., and Wright, L., Families and Chronic Illness: Assumptions, Assessment, and Intervention. In Loraine Wright and Maureen Leahey (eds.), *Families and Chronic Illness,* Springhouse, PA: Springhouse Corporation, 1987, pp. 55-75.

8. Rolland, J., Chronic Illness and the Family: An Overview. In Loraine Wright and Maureen Leahey (eds.), *Families and Chronic Illness,* Springhouse, PA: Springhouse Corporation, 1987, pp. 33-54.

9. *Ibid.,* p. 46.

10. Laframboise, H., Health Policy: Breaking the Problem Down into More Manageable Segments. *Canadian Medical Association Journal,* 108, February, 1973, pp. 388-393.

11. Dever, G., *Community Health Analysis.* Rockville, MD: Aspen Systems Corporation, 1980.

12. Levin, J., and Vanderpool, H., Religious Factors in Physical Health and the Prevention of Illness. *Prevention in Human Services,* 9, 2, 1991, pp. 41-64.

13. Matarazzo, J., Behavioral Immunogens and Pathogens in Health and Illness. In C. Scheirer and B. Hammond (eds.), *Psychology in Health,* Washington, DC: American Psychological Association, 3, 1984.

14. Bandura, A., *Social Learning Theory,* Englewood Cliff, NJ: Prentice-Hall, 1977.

15. Green, L., Erikson, M.P., and Schor, E., Preventive in Health and Illness. In C. Scheirer and B. Hammond (eds.), *Psychology in Health,* Washington, DC: American Psychological Association, 3, 1984, CHECK

16. Milsum, J.H., *Health, Stress, and Illness.* New York: Praeger Publications, 1984.

17. Bird, L., Christie-Seely, J., and Yaremko-Dolan, M., Value Systems and the Family. In Janet Christie-Seely (ed.), *Working with the Family in Primary Care.* Praeger, 1984, p. 96.

18. The original version of this section on prevention first appeared in: McBride, J., The Partnership Between Behavioral and Preventive Medicine, *Journal of the Medical Association of Georgia,* 85, 1996, pp. 153-155. Used by permission.

19. Levin and Vanderpool, *op. cit.,* p. 51.

20. Hill, P., and Butler, E., The Role of Religion in Promoting Physical Health, *Journal of Psychology and Christianity,* 14, 2, 1995, p. 141.

21. Larson, B., *There Is More to Health Than Not Being Sick,* Waco, TX: Word Books, 1981.

22. Frankl, V., *Man's Search for Meaning.* Boston: Beacon Press, 1963.

23. Proverbs 3:7, 8.

Chapter 10

1. Hoffer, E. *The True Believer,* New York: Harper and Row, 1951.
2. Schaef, A., and Fassel, D., *The Addictive Organization.* San Francisco: Harper and Row, 1988, pp. 57-76.
3. Tony Campolo, Introduction. In John Fischer (author), *Real Christians Dance,* Minneapolis: Bethany House, 1988.

Chapter 11

1. Carson, R., and Butcher, J., *Abnormal Psychology and Modern Life.* Ninth Edition, New York: Harper and Row, 1992.
2. Oates, W., *Behind the Masks.* Philadelphia: Westminster Press, 1987, p. 11.
3. Marsh, D., *Families with Mental Illness: New Directions for in Professional Practice.* New York: Praeger, 1992.
4. McCannon, J., *Journal of Pastoral Care,* Fall, 1991, p. 213.
5. Govig, S., Chronic Mental Illness and the Family: Contexts for Pastoral Care. *The Journal of Pastoral Care,* 1993, 47, 4, pp. 405-418.
6. Raup, C., An Analysis of Seven Concepts Related to Pathology Which Are Common to Psychology and Theology. *Journal of Psychology and Christianity,* 1989, 8, 2, pp. 5-12.
7. Pruyser, P., *The Minister as Diagnostician.* Philadelphia: Westminster Press, 1976, pp. 60-79.
8. Oates, W., *The Religious Care of the Psychiatric Patient.* Philadelphia: Westminster Press, 1978, pp. 108-109.
9. Wise, C., *The Meaning of Pastoral Care.* Bloomington, IL: Meyer Stone Books, 1989.
10. Knight, J., *A Psychiatrist Looks at Religion and Health.* Nashville: Abingston Press, 1964, p. 85.
11. *Ibid.,* p. 85.
12. *Ibid.,* p. 85.
13. Clebsch, W., and Jaekle, C., *Pastoral Care in Historical Perspective.* Northvale, NJ: Jason Aronson Publishers, 1964, p. 4.
14. Berger, P., and Luckmann, T., *The Social Construction of Reality.* New York: Doubleday, 1966, p. 86.
15. Garland, J., and Conrad, A., The Church as a Context of Professional Practice. In D.S.R. Garland and D.L. Pancoast (eds.), *The Church's Ministry with Families: A Practical Guide* (pp. 71-87). Waco: Word, 1990, p. 80.
16. Philippians 4:8.
17. Framo, J., The Integration of Marital Therapy with Sessions with Family of Origin. In Alan Gurman and David Kniskern (eds.), *Handbook of Family Therapy,* 1981, pp. 133-158.
18. Matthew 7:5.
19. Frankl, V., *Man's Search for Meaning.* Boston: Beacon Press, 1963.
20. Seligman, M., *Learned Optimism.* New York: Simon & Schuster (Pocket Book Edition), 1990, p. 7.

21. Nelson, W., *Liberation.* Chicago: Covenant Publications, 1974, pp. 1, 7.

22. Matthew 6:34.

23. Matthew 28:20.

24. Tillich, P., *The Courage to Be.* New York: Vail-Ballou Press, Inc., 1952.

25. *Ibid.,* p. 62.

26. Oates, 1987, *op. cit.,* p. 43.

27. Narramore, S., *No Condemnation.* Grand Rapids, MI: Zondervan Publishing House, 1984.

28. *Ibid.,* p. 165.

29. Langer, E., Mindfulness, *American Health,* March 1990, p. 56.

30. Brinsmead, R., *The Christian Verdict,* Essay Eight, 1983, p. 5.

31. Langer, E., *Mindfulness,* Reading, MA: Addison-Wesley Publishing Company, 1989.

32. Oates, *op. cit.,* 1978, pp. 222-233.

33. Xavier, N., *The Two Faces of Religion,* Tuscaloosa, AL: Portals Press, 1987.

Chapter 12

1. Ecclesiastes 1:2-3.

2. Clinebell, H., *Basic Types of Pastoral Counseling.* Nashville: Abington Press, 1966.

3. Berger, L., *From Instinct to Identity: The Development of Personality.* Englewood, CA: Prentice-Hall, Inc., 1974, p. 329.

4. *Ibid.,* p. 331.

5. Gerkin, C., *Crisis Experience in Modern Life.* Nashville: Abington Press, 1979.

6. Berger, *op. cit.*

7. DeAngelis, B., *Real Moments.* New York: Delacorte Press, 1994, p. 90.

8. Learner, H., *The Dance of Anger.* New York: Harper and Row, 1985.

9. Hoffman, V., *The Codependent Church.* New York: Crossroads Publishing Company, 1991, p. 15.

10. Hogg, J., and Frank, M., Toward an Interpersonal Model of Codependence and Contradependence. *Journal of Counseling and Development,* 70, 1992, pp. 371-375.

11. Mason, M., *Making Our Lives Our Own.* San Francisco: Harper and Row, 1991, p. 98.

12. van Rooyen, S., *How to Love the Church: Breaking the Cycle of Co-Dependency.* Sermon given at The Association of Adventist Forums, June 1990.

13. Loughlin, G., *Telling God's Story: Bible, Church, and Narrative Theology.* New York:Cambridge University Press, 1996, p. 73.

14. Hogg, *Ibid.,* p. 372.

15. Saari, C., Relationship Factors in the Creation of Identity. In Hugh Rosen and Kevin Kuehlwein (eds.), *Constructing Realities,* San Francisco: Jossey-Bass Publishers, 1996, pp. 141-166.

16. Gerkin, *op. cit.,* p. 207.

17. Kaeo, C., Identity, Faith, and Maturity. *Journal of Psychology and Theology,* 3, 1, 1975, pp. 43-48.

18. Hillman, J., *The Soul's Code.* New York: Random House, 1996, p. 6.

19. Shuller, R., *Self-Esteem: The New Reformation,* Waco, TX: Word Books, 1982, p. 162.

20. Gerkin, *op. cit.,* p. 215.

21. Kao. *op. cit.,* p. 44.

22. Kass, J., *Contributions of Religious Experience to Psychological and Physical Well-Being: Research Evidence and an Explanatory Model. The Caregiver Journal,* 8, 4, 1991, pp. 4-11.

23. Kass, *Ibid.,* p. 11.

24. Narramore, S., *No Condemnation,* Grand Rapids: Zonderman Publishing House, p. 298.

25. *Ibid.*

26. Childs, J., *Ethics in Business,* Minneapolis: Augsberg Fortress Press, 1995, p. 20.

27. *Ibid.,* p. 19.

28. Covey, S., *The Seven Habits of Highly Effective People.* New York: Simon & Schuster Inc. (First Fireside Edition), 1990, p. 241.

29. Ephesians 2:19, Revised Standard Version.

Chapter 13

1. Rubin, L., *Families on the Fault Line.* New York: Harper Collins Publishers, 1994, chapter 3.

2. Braaten, C., *Christ and Counter-Christ.* Philadelphia: Fortress Press, 1971, p. 91.

3. Xavier, N., *The Two Faces of Religion,* Tuscaloosa, AL: Portal Press, 1981.

4. *Ibid.,* p. 54.

5. Rosen, H., Meaning-Making Narratives. In Hugh Rosen and Kevin Kuehlwein (eds.), *Constructing Realities: Meaning Making Perspectives for Psychotherapists,* San Francisco: Jossey-Bass Publishers, 1996, p. 23.

6 Hauerwas, S., and Burrell, D., From System to Story: An Alternative Pattern for Rationality in Ethics. In Stanley Hauerwas and Gregory Jones (eds.), *Why Narrative?,* Grand Rapids: William B. Eerdmans Publishing Company, 1989, pp. 158-190.

7. Borg, M., *Meeting Jesus Again for the First Time,* San Francisco: Harper-Collins, 1995. While not agreeing with all of Borg's conclusions, I have appreciated his insights.

8. *Ibid.*

9. *Ibid.,* p. 121.

10. Hauerwas, S., A Community of Character. Notre Dame: University of Notre Dame Press, 1981, pp. 53, 59.

11. Freedman, J., and Combs, G., *Narrative Therapy,* New York: Norton & Company, 1996, p. 22.

12. *Ibid.,* pp. 29, 30.

13. *Ibid.,* p. 35.

14. Rosen, H., *op. cit.,* p. 39.

15. Brinsmead, R., *Judged by the Gospel*, Fallbrook, CA: Verdict Publications, 1980, p. 209.

16. Crandal, A., Christian Ethics, *Evangelica,* St. Joseph, MI: Evangelica Publications, 2, 2, 1981, p. 26.

17. Brinsmead, R., A Critique of Christian Nomism, *The Christian Verdict,* Special Issue 1, 1983, p. 9.

18. *Ibid.*

19. *Ibid.,* p. 240.

20. Luke 10:30-37.

21. Brinsmead, *op. cit.,* p. 245.

Chapter 14

1. Figley, C. (ed.), *Compassion Fatigue: Coping with Secondary Traumatic Stress Disorder in Those Who Treat the Traumatized.* New York: Brunner/Mazel, 1995.

2. Thayer, N., *Spirituality and Pastoral Care.* Philadelphia: Fortress, 1985.

3. Whitfield, C., *Alcoholism, Attachments, and Spirituality.* New Jersey: Perrin, Inc., 1985.

4. Heidegger, M., *Being and Time.* New York: Harper and Row, 1962.

5. Frankl, V., *Man's Search for Meaning.* Boston: Beacon Press, 1963.

6. Tillich, P., *The Courage to Be.* New Haven, CT: Yale University Press, 1952.

7. Jung, C., *Modern Man in Search of a Soul,* New York: Harcourt Jovanovich, 1933.

8. Mitchell, K., Editorial. *The Journal of Pastoral Care,* 43, 2, 1989, p. 94.

9. Maeder, T., Wounded Healers. *The Atlantic Monthly,* January, 1989.

Index

Page numbers followed by the letter "f indicate figures; those followed by the letter "t" indicate tables.

Order Your Own Copy of
This Important Book for Your Personal Library!

SPIRITUAL CRISIS
Surviving Trauma to the Soul

_____ in hardbound at $39.95 (ISBN: 0-7890-0135-7)

_____ in softbound at $19.95 (ISBN: 0-7890-0460-7)

COST OF BOOKS_____

OUTSIDE USA/CANADA/
MEXICO: ADD 20%_____

POSTAGE & HANDLING_____
(US: $3.00 for first book & $1.25
for each additional book)
Outside US: $4.75 for first book
& $1.75 for each additional book)

SUBTOTAL_____

IN CANADA: ADD 7% GST_____

STATE TAX_____
(NY, OH & MN residents, please
add appropriate local sales tax)

FINAL TOTAL_____
(If paying in Canadian funds,
convert using the current
exchange rate. UNESCO
coupons welcome.)

☐ **BILL ME LATER:** ($5 service charge will be added)
(Bill-me option is good on US/Canada/Mexico orders only;
not good to jobbers, wholesalers, or subscription agencies.)

☐ Check here if billing address is different from
shipping address and attach purchase order and
billing address information.

Signature_____

☐ **PAYMENT ENCLOSED: $**_____

☐ **PLEASE CHARGE TO MY CREDIT CARD.**

☐ Visa   ☐ MasterCard   ☐ AmEx   ☐ Discover
☐ Diner's Club

Account # _____

Exp. Date _____

Signature _____

Prices in US dollars and subject to change without notice.

NAME _____

INSTITUTION _____

ADDRESS _____

CITY _____

STATE/ZIP _____

COUNTRY _____ COUNTY (NY residents only) _____

TEL _____ FAX _____

E-MAIL_____
May we use your e-mail address for confirmations and other types of information? ☐ Yes   ☐ No

Order From Your Local Bookstore or Directly From
The Haworth Press, Inc.
10 Alice Street, Binghamton, New York 13904-1580 • USA
TELEPHONE: 1-800-HAWORTH (1-800-429-6784) / Outside US/Canada: (607) 722-5857
FAX: 1-800-895-0582 / Outside US/Canada: (607) 772-6362
E-mail: getinfo@haworth.com
PLEASE PHOTOCOPY THIS FORM FOR YOUR PERSONAL USE.

BOF96